05

AUGUST 22, 2018

"SHOOTING STAR" IS RELEASED DURING THE KOREAN OVERWATCH FAN FESTIVAL.

NOVEMBER 2, 2018

"REUNION" AND THE ASHE ORIGIN STORY ARE REVEALED AT BLIZZCON.

06

DECEMBER 18, 2018

"COOKIEWATCH" IS RELEASED.

FEBRUARY 25, 2019

THE BAPTISTE ORIGIN STORY IS RELEASED.

APRIL 16, 2019

THE "STORM RISING" CINEMATICS ARE REVEALED AS PART OF THE THIRD OVERWATCH ARCHIVES EVENT.

07

JULY 22, 2019

THE SIGMA ORIGIN STORY IS RELEASED.

NOVEMBER 1, 2019

"ZERO HOUR" IS REVEALED AT BLIZZCON.

MARCH 18, 2020

THE ECHO ORIGIN STORY IS RELEASED.

ARMS

# THE CINEMATIC ART OF

# OVERWATCH®

VOLUME 2
2017-2020

TITAN BOOKS

BLIZZARD ENTERTAINMENT

# INTRODUCTION

ONE

**WHEN *OVERWATCH* LAUNCHED IN 2016, IT WON INDUSTRY ACCOLADES AND A HUGE INTERNATIONAL COMMUNITY FORMED AROUND IT. PLAYERS QUICKLY IDENTIFIED WITH** their favorite heroes and developed visceral, personal attachments to them. Meanwhile, the characters began to evolve in game with new skins, dialogue, and events.

While the lore of the universe was engaging, it quickly became apparent that the main hook was the heroes, who exploded across media including cinematics, comics, online content, and the game itself. "People really seemed drawn to these characters," said creative director & vice president of story and franchise development Jeff Chamberlain. "We wanted to acknowledge that and create more stories to share with the world. It's always been a goal in Overwatch to tell emotionally engaging, character-based stories."

LEFT Color key from the "Reunion" animated short.

The first batch of Overwatch's cinematics, starting with the game's announcement in 2014, had introduced these characters to the world through prerendered shorts and 2.5D motion stories. But for the next wave of films, the team decided to explore the diverse cast by branching out into 2D anime, in-game cinematics (IGCs) rendered in the game engine, and stop-motion animation. "All the different forms of media we could use are just different ways to tell more story. And that's ultimately what our goal is," said Chamberlain.

**TOP LEFT** Layout drawing for the Doomfist origin story.

**TOP RIGHT** In-progress illustration from the "Retribution" 2.5D motion-story outro.

**ABOVE** Storyboard of Mina Liao from the Echo origin story.

**OPPOSITE** Color key featuring Tracer's hoverbike from the "Storm Rising" in-game cinematic.

## A GREAT CONVERGENCE

Apart from just telling more stories in new formats, the team wanted to bring what audiences see in the cinematics and what they experience in the game together as much as possible. This was a goal that the filmmakers had been pursuing from the beginning.

Take the example of Tracer. "In the original announcement cinematic, which was done in the Blizzard film pipeline, Tracer looks nothing like what she looks like in the game," said Jim Jiang, the CG supervisor for in-game cinematics. "Her limbs are longer, everything's exaggerated, her face is different. Progressively, we ended up dialing those changes back to get closer to the actual game model because we wanted to make sure it didn't look like we recast a different actor. We wanted to keep it really consistent."

To achieve an even more unified look, the team used game assets as much as possible for the 3D films. This strategy is the foundation of the IGCs, which are rendered using the game engine. "The goal is to use only game assets to drive the IGCs," said Jiang. "All the effects and maps and everything are entirely from the game."

For stop-motion animation, 2.5D motion stories, and 2D anime, the creators also found ways to achieve cohesion between the different media. They drew on core art pillars, infusing the films with the handcrafted feel, dynamic animation, and vibrant colors that define the Overwatch aesthetic.

39

## FREEDOM TO EXPLORE

Using the various cinematic styles and production methodologies at their disposal, the Overwatch team would engage in an adaptive approach to creating its newest cinematic content. They would embrace change, develop confidence as they overcame challenges, and create new ways of working.

As they moved forward, Overwatch's creators wouldn't be afraid to build new pipelines or use different media to develop their growing cast of characters—they would remain open to experimentation and would keep trying new things that would allow them to expand the cast and the universe.

"With Overwatch, we try to create universally appealing stories that can be told in any medium," said Chamberlain. "So the idea of moving into something like anime for Overwatch, in my mind, was a no-brainer. I could see us doing more of that in the future. And the stop-motion was the brainchild of Justin Rasch, one of our animators, and his passion for the medium. He came in with a pitch one day, and we thought, 'That'd be so cool. We can't not do that.'

"If there's a passionate artistic idea that supports the universe, then why not? Why not chase that? Because if we're excited about it, then chances are our audience is going to be excited about it as well."

**RIGHT** In-progress shot from the "Trace & Bake" stop-motion animation.

OVER

# ANIMATED SHORTS

TWO

**THE FIRST WAVE OF OVERWATCH'S PRERENDERED 3D CINEMATICS WAS MAINLY FOCUSED ON BUILDING EXCITEMENT FOR THE GAME'S RELEASE IN 2016.** After achieving that major milestone, the Overwatch team took a moment to reconsider what they wanted to accomplish with animated shorts and how they planned to work on them. It was almost ten months between the release of "Infiltration" at BlizzCon 2016 and the next release, "Rise and Shine," on August 23, 2017.

This pause allowed the team to reflect on the prerendered cinematics they had made to date and to enhance their focus on character, story, and quality. "If you look at the first episodes, it was really a question of how we were going to do them," said senior producer Kevin VanderJagt. "But once we worked out the kinks in our process, it really let us focus on plussing things."

The next phase of animated shorts that began with "Rise and Shine" required some careful orchestration, as the cinematics were designed to show how different heroes responded to Winston's recall to reform

LEFT Final render of McCree opening the payload that contains Echo in "Reunion."

Overwatch. The culmination of these narrative arcs eventually became the premise for announcing *Overwatch 2*. "That had always been our goal from day one when we did 'Recall'—we wanted to get the team back together," said creative director & vice president of story and franchise development Jeff Chamberlain. "We didn't really know whether or not that was going to coincide with *Overwatch 2* at the time, but that idea was brought up pretty early on."

The team wanted to balance this strong narrative agenda, though, with a focus on character, which they had seen great responses to in the first wave of animated shorts. "Because of the success of shorts like 'Dragons,' we felt like that was the direction to go in—to explore characters rather than plot," said Arnold Tsang, *Overwatch*'s character art director. "But we did try to tie in Winston's recall organically in each of the stories."

"A lot of the focus is on setting up where characters are in proximity to Winston's recall," said VanderJagt. "Most of the cinematics are very much a reaction to that; they're trying to establish where these characters are emotionally and how and why they respond to Winston's plea to reform the Overwatch team."

"Each person reacted differently," said principal writer Andrew Robinson. "And in their reaction, we got insight into who they are. That's why each piece resonates so differently, because they are different personalities. For Reinhardt, it's a moral imperative: 'We have to do this.' McCree is like, 'I might not be the right guy anymore.' And Mei is thrilled at the chance to be a part of it: 'I'm all in.'"

**TOP RIGHT** Storyboard of Mei looking at the drive that contains her research from "Rise and Shine."

**MIDDLE RIGHT** Storyboard of Reinhardt and Balderich at the bar in "Honor and Glory."

**BOTTOM RIGHT** Color key of Dae-hyun and D.Va from "Shooting Star."

## SHARED ASSETS

The next phase of animated shorts wasn't just designed to bring the characters together; it was also an opportunity to heighten the convergence between game and cinematics.

Following the launch of *Overwatch* in 2016, new game content was released at a regular clip. Because the game and cinematics attempted to share assets as much as possible, every new map meant another location where a story could take place, and every new in-game object introduced more set-dressing possibilities.

"In order to make these shorts, we'll try to reuse as much as we can from the game," said director Ben Dai. "It's a no-brainer when we have the assets already built for us. We absolutely capitalize on those, and it works out really well."

Reciprocally, costumes, vehicles, and even characters were made or modified specifically for cinematics and then introduced into the game. "The majority of episodes after launch had either key characters and costume designs that did not originate with the game, or added to sets and environments that were very early work-in-progress from the game," said VanderJagt. "The level of communication, the amount of asset sharing, and the mystic synchronization we had to have with one another was more complicated than on the first episodes."

This collaboration was particularly critical around game maps, which both serve as the settings for the cinematic stories and can be explored by players in the game. "From 'Recall' on, we decided to see how closely we could keep the environments consistent," said *Overwatch*'s assistant art director, Dion Rogers. "It makes the world feel alive and evolving."

This connection became so integral that the *Overwatch* map designers began, in a way, to serve as location scouts for the films. "Once we had established an early version of a map, we would have meetings with the team working on the cinematic and give them suggestions for where a scene could fit," said Rogers. "Working this way together made it a lot easier to respect the gameplay needs and accommodate the cinematic at the same time."

**TOP LEFT** Storyboard of D.Va celebrating an eSports victory from "Shooting Star."

**BOTTOM LEFT** In-progress art from the title sequence of "Reunion."

**RIGHT** Sketch of Busan from "Shooting Star."

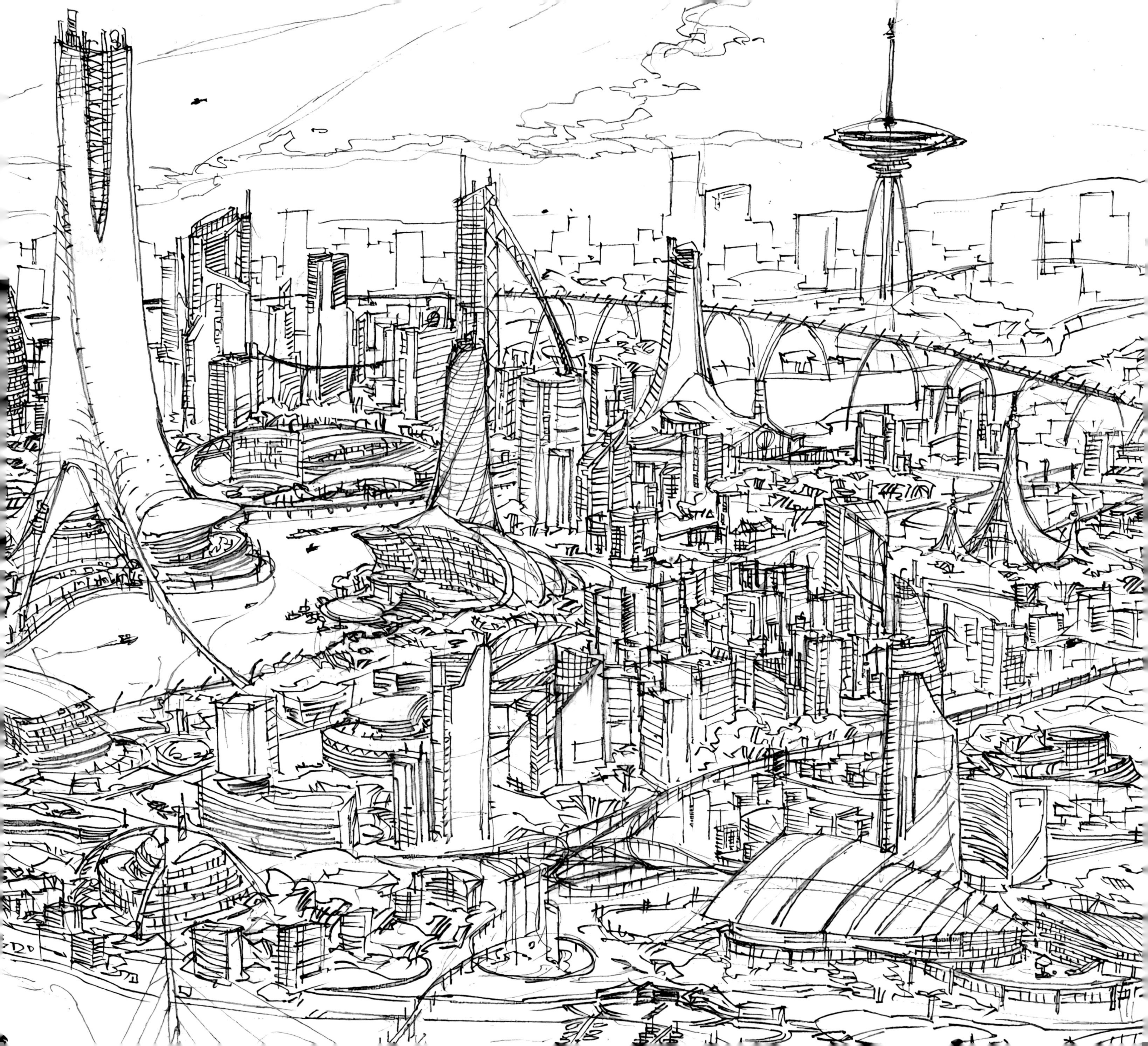

# RISE AND SHINE

"YES, WINSTON. I AM WITH YOU."

—MEI

**RIGHT** Final render of Mei from "Rise and Shine."

## WITH "RISE AND SHINE," RELEASED ON AUGUST 23, 2017,

the Overwatch team chose to center a cinematic around Mei, a hero who doesn't wield typical superpowers. "We wanted to put forth the thought that she has to use science to overcome her situation," said principal writer Andrew Robinson, who wrote the short. "She discovers that science is her superpower, which enables her to act on her motivation to help save the world."

To show this hero's journey, the filmmakers had to take Mei through a grueling test—to break her down so that she could build herself back up. During the course of the film, she loses all of her colleagues, along with nine years of her life, after her team of researchers enter a cryogenic sleep to wait out a storm that hits Ecopoint: Antarctica. "We wanted to put Mei through an emotional

## MEI'S EVOLUTION

To show how far Mei comes in the piece, the filmmakers had to establish who she was at the start. This required beginning the story nine years prior to when Mei receives Winston's recall message—with the moment when her cryogenic sleep begins.

At the start of the film, Mei is shooting a video diary that explains why she and her colleagues have to go into hibernation. During the course of the recording, the viewer gets a sense of Mei's upbeat yet unassuming personality, as well as where she fits in with her group of coworkers. "We decided early on that she's sort of like the kid in the group, like everyone sort of takes care of her," said Dai. "She's a brilliant scientist, but imagine this is her first job. So it makes sense that during the whole sequence, where everyone's packing up and getting ready for the hibernation, she's still doing her video."

crucible," said Robinson. "So we took everything we could from her, and she still stood up. And that is a hero. She lost her friends. She lost her connection to the world. She lost time. She lost the opportunity to do things she wanted to do. And she said, 'No, I'm going to find a way to get all that back.'"

Telling a tale like this was a big risk. Developing the concept meant committing to making a film without much action, which had been a staple of previous prerendered cinematics. It also meant planning a significantly longer piece—"Rise and Shine" is just short of nine minutes long—so that they could show the different stages of Mei's grief and evolution. "We were given a lot of leeway," said director Ben Dai. "The most important thing is to tell a compelling story. And because there wasn't a lot of action—it's just Mei and Snowball most of the time—it was possible to make the show longer."

This willingness to forego action and focus on character and emotion was a stimulating departure for the creators. "The idea that we could tell a compelling story with no action in it whatsoever was so emotionally rewarding," said Robinson.

**OPPOSITE** Concepts of the Ecopoint: Antarctica team of scientists.

**THIS PAGE** Storyboards depicting key moments in "Rise and Shine."

## MEI AND SNOWBALL

Most of Mei's evolution is played out with her companion robot, Snowball, who was a tough character to crack, as there was always the danger that he could become gimmicky. "We tried to make it so that Snowball definitely is a character," said Dai. "He's sort of like Mei's safety blanket. And we tried to build up their relationship for that final moment when Snowball sacrifices himself."

To develop Snowball's relationship with Mei, the storyboard artists depicted day-to-day interactions the characters might have with one another. "Sometimes, what we do in the beginning stages is explore character relationships," said principal storyboard artist Mike Koizumi. "So we did drawings of Mei waking up that showed how Snowball helps her. Like she's leaning on him. She's sleepy. Does he push her slippers over to her so she can step in?"

One of the key moments the storyboard artists hit upon during these explorations was the high five between Mei and Snowball. "That moment of them high-fiving is the pinnacle to me," said Dai. "It's like the magical moment where she really connects with that little robot, which makes the loss of him even harder for her to swallow."

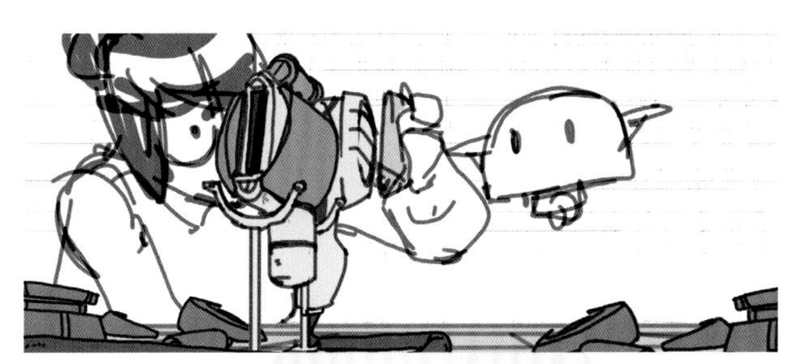

The depiction of Mei's Endothermic Blaster in "Rise and Shine" fits the overall tone of the piece, which emphasizes discovery and innovation over conflict and combat. "She wasn't building her weapon to take out an opposing team," said director of story George Krstic. "She was building it to get through a problem. She was using intellect to overcome challenges."

**OPPOSITE** In-progress concepts and storyboards of Snowball.

**THIS PAGE** Storyboards exploring how Mei and Snowball could interact with one another while Mei builds her blaster.

TEA STATION
OOLONG

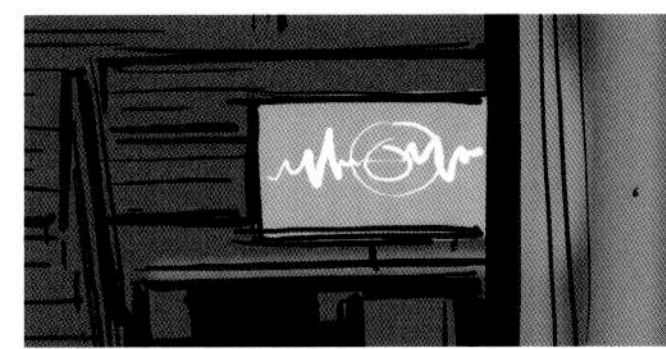

## TEA TIME

Another big emotional arc in "Rise and Shine" concerns Mei's relationship with her coworkers, none of whom emerge from their cryogenic sleep. Mei's realization that they've all died is a dramatic surprise brought home via an everyday activity—making tea for the group. "We tried to tell the story of how she's the one that gets up first thing in the morning and makes tea for everybody else," said Dai. "So it's natural that after the hibernation, she gets up and makes tea for them."

Then, at the end of the piece, before Mei embarks upon her journey into the outside world, she makes tea for her dead colleagues one last time. Senior storyboard artist Ted Boonthanakit landed on this idea while he was considering how Mei might say goodbye. "We had been discussing earlier on in the script when she was planning to make tea for the team," said Boonthanakit. "So I thought, 'Why don't we bring that back and bring it all together at the very end?' I didn't realize it would have that kind of an impact until I started sketching out that shot."

"It's a wonderful moment," said Robinson. "Not only does she honor them, but she also takes them with her. In a way, she's saving the memory of them by not giving up."

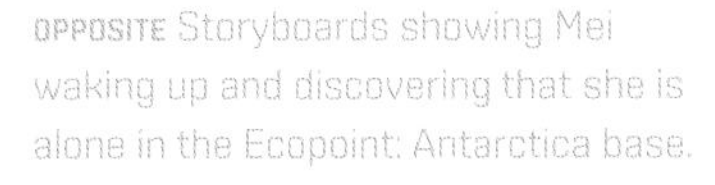

**OPPOSITE** Storyboards showing Mei waking up and discovering that she is alone in the Ecopoint: Antarctica base.

**TOP** Storyboards from key moments in the short.

**ABOVE** Concepts of the mugs belonging to the Ecopoint: Antarctica scientists.

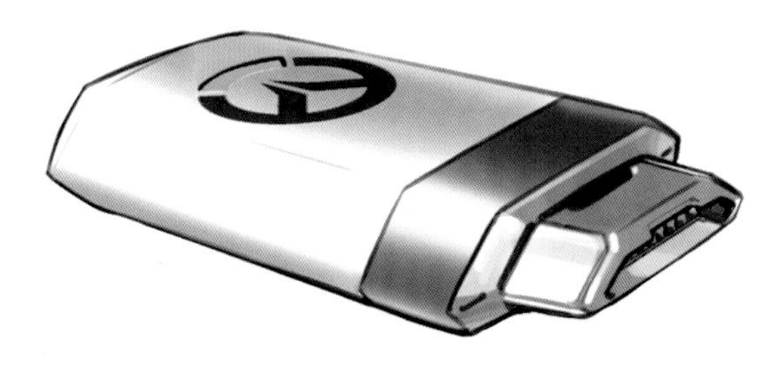

## THE STORY IN THE MAP

▲ The development of "Rise and Shine" coincided with the unveiling of a new map called Ecopoint: Antarctica. One of the goals of the short was to imbue this in-game location with story-based significance.

"We were fortunate enough to have the map mostly done when we started working on the cinematic," said Dai. "So we flew around in the map and picked out locations—like the shots in the kitchen, where she first wakes up and brushes her teeth, and the cryogenic room where they fall asleep. And in the level, there was a radio tower that looked broken. So that was the inspiration for the obstacle that she needed to overcome."

"As we started to learn more of the cinematic story, we thought about what it would be like when the base was fully functional—how life was for the different people working there," said Dion Rogers, *Overwatch*'s assistant art director. "Mei is a very positive character, so we put up posters like 'Hang In There.' And you can tell which desk is hers because it has a tea set and her flip-flops next to it. And then on one side of the base, we made a digital wall that has a beach setting on it. All of these ideas came from the question, 'If you were a worker here and you needed to stay here for months, how would you make the space comfortable for yourself?'" ▼

**LEFT, TOP & OPPOSITE** Paint overs of in-game art for the Ecopoint: Antarctica base.

**ABOVE** Concept of the drive containing Mei's research.

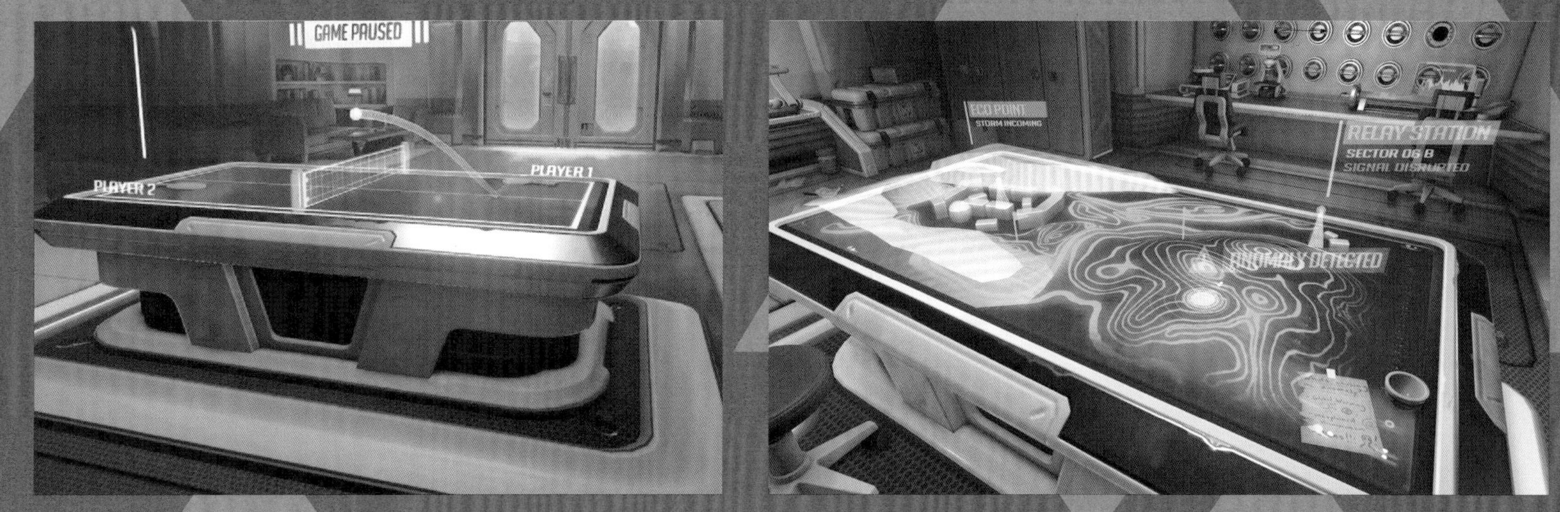
GAME PAUSED
PLAYER 2
PLAYER 1
ECO POINT
STORM INCOMING
RELAY STATION
SECTOR 06 B
SIGNAL DISRUPTED
ANOMALY DETECTED

TEMPERATURE
STORM ALERT!
MONITORING SYSTEM
RADIO STATION
SECTOR 45 A
SECTOR 38 B
SECTOR 09 B
WEATHER
A
B
STORM INCOMING
-43°C
ECO POINT
ANOMALY DETECTED
RELAY STATION
SECTOR 06 B
SIGNAL DISRUPTED

## WARM COLORS

▲ "Rise and Shine" takes place in an Antarctic base surrounded by ice and snow. This made blue and white obvious choices for the dominant colors in the piece, and the filmmakers gave everything a blue tint.

Blue and white, though, can feel cold and detached, which didn't fit the arc of Mei's character or her fundamentally cheerful personality. "The show starts with a mostly somber and cold mood to emphasize Mei's loneliness while the rest of her crew has perished," said former art director Mathias Verhasselt. "Toward the end of the show, as Mei is driven to hear Winston's message of hope, there is a progression from a beautiful warm sunset lighting toward a magical green aurora australis."

The most striking warm-color contrast to the blue-and-white environment is Mei's red snow outfit, which she dons to climb the tower that allows her to communicate with the outside world. "It's a good, solid warm red that makes her pop out from the landscape," said senior director of Blizzard Animation Steven Chen. ▼

Both Mei's pajama outfit and her subzero gear were costumes made for "Rise and Shine," which subsequently became skins in the game. Then, on "Zero Hour," the trailer that announced *Overwatch 2*, Mei was given her new look. As a result, Mei never appears in an Overwatch cinematic wearing her original in-game outfit.

**OPPOSITE** Costume studies for Mei.

**THIS PAGE** In-progress versions of Mei's Endothermic Blaster (right) and ammo cartridge (left).

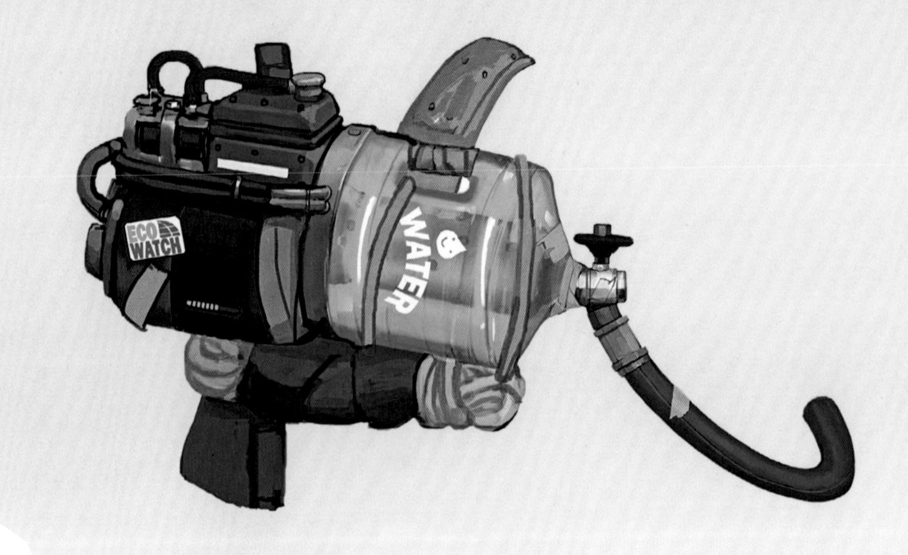

**TOP** Storyboard of Mei venturing out into the Antarctic wasteland.

**LEFT, RIGHT & OPPOSITE** Concepts, storyboard, and final render showcasing Mei's backpack, which includes solar panels for charging Snowball.

### *THE RIGHT ICE*

▲ Creating modest amounts of ice is difficult to do well in CG animation. "Rise and Shine" upped the ante significantly by taking place in a nearly all-ice environment and featuring a character whose main abilities revolve around freezing things. "There was a lot of iteration to find the right balance of color in the ice because there's always this green or blue tint to ice in the real world," said Chen. "If you do it too much, it looks like there's blue dye in the ice."

The filmmakers also had to take into account how ice was depicted in the game when it came to both the Ecopoint: Antarctica environment and Mei's ice-driven abilities. "We had to straddle the line between what the game has in it and what ice looks like in real life to find a middle ground that fit the animation style and also fit the game universe," said Dai. ▼

**RIGHT** Final render of Mei shooting ice from her Endothermic Blaster.

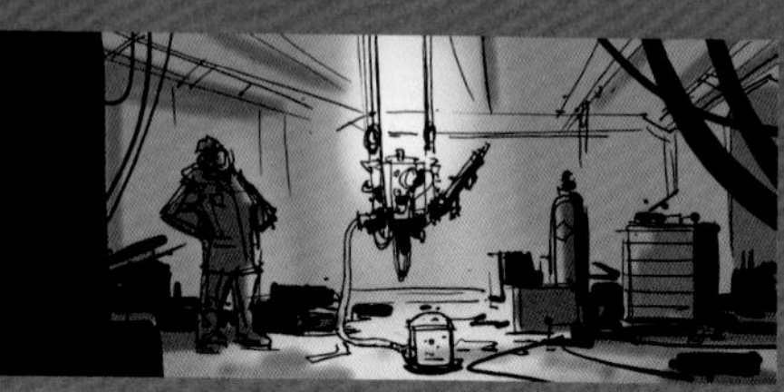

**THESE PAGES** Early storyboards exploring how Mei might scale the radio tower and navigate the Antarctic landscape.

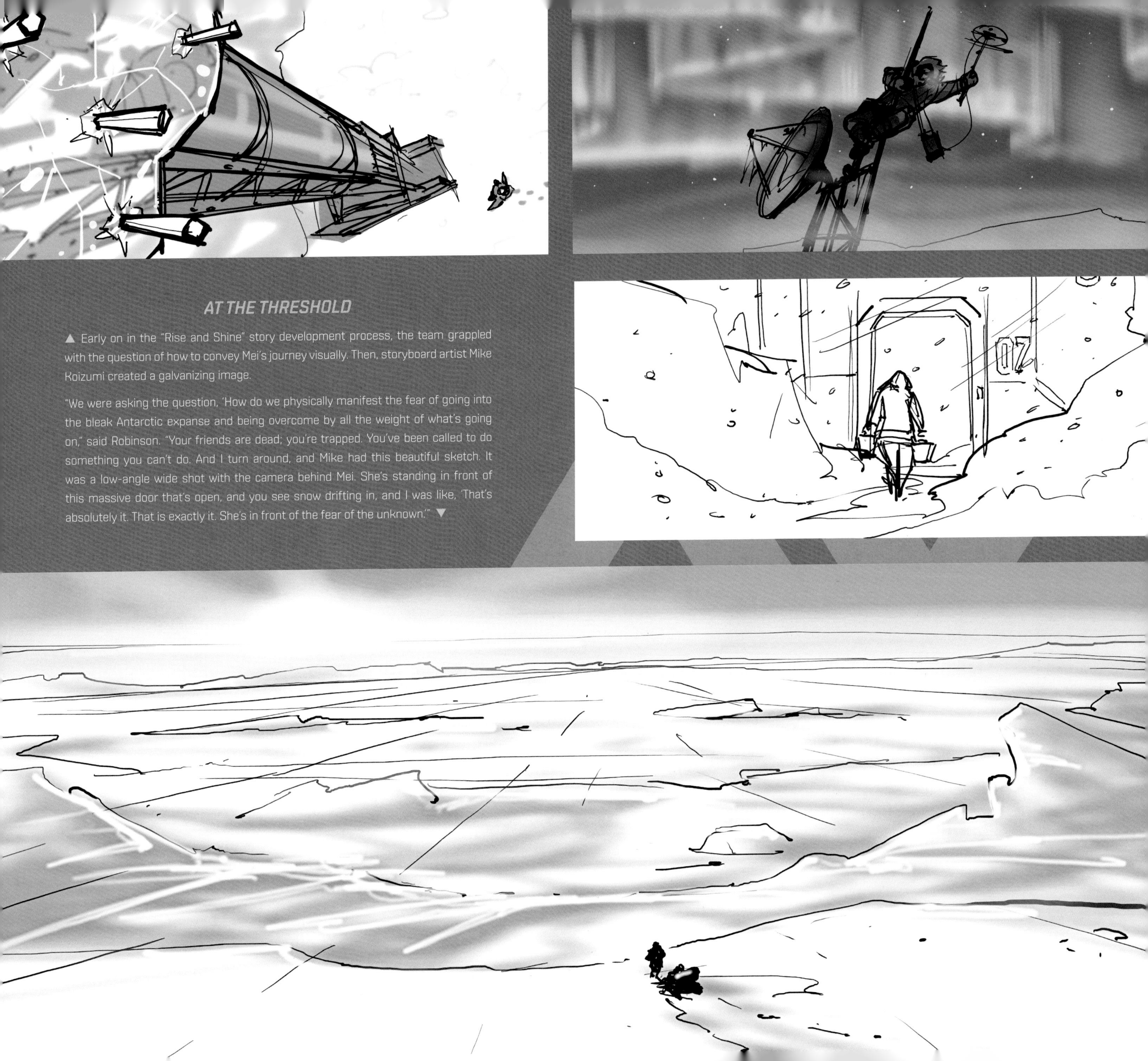


## AT THE THRESHOLD

▲ Early on in the "Rise and Shine" story development process, the team grappled with the question of how to convey Mei's journey visually. Then, storyboard artist Mike Koizumi created a galvanizing image.

"We were asking the question, 'How do we physically manifest the fear of going into the bleak Antarctic expanse and being overcome by all the weight of what's going on," said Robinson. "Your friends are dead; you're trapped. You've been called to do something you can't do. And I turn around, and Mike had this beautiful sketch. It was a low-angle wide shot with the camera behind Mei. She's standing in front of this massive door that's open, and you see snow drifting in, and I was like, 'That's absolutely it. That is exactly it. She's in front of the fear of the unknown.'" ▼

**PREVIOUS PAGES** Final render of Mei gazing at the Southern Lights from the top of the radio tower.

**RIGHT** Final render of Mei embarking on her journey across Antarctica and back to civilization.

# HONOR AND GLORY

"I HAVE BEEN CALLED.
I MUST ANSWER."

—REINHARDT

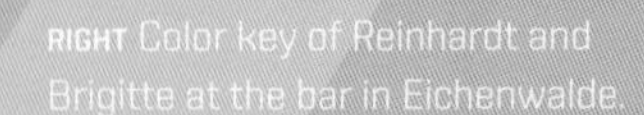

**RIGHT** Color key of Reinhardt and Brigitte at the bar in Eichenwalde.

## FOR MANY ON THE OVERWATCH TEAM, "HONOR AND GLORY"

—released on November 3, 2017, at BlizzCon—is a shining example of how everything came together to produce a cinematic that resembles the image they had in their minds' eyes. "'Honor and Glory' was the first time it was really all about execution," said animation supervisor Hunter Grant. "We weren't figuring anything out anymore; there wasn't anything in that piece that we didn't know how to do. It was all about, 'How do we make this performance the best it can be?'"

The core of "Honor and Glory" is Reinhardt's character arc, which takes him from shallow glory hound to honor-bound Crusader. "In game he comes off as someone who doesn't seem like he's thinking everything through: he just jumps in with both feet all the time," said creative director & vice president of story and franchise development Jeff Chamberlain.

Reinhardt's drive—and his maturation as a character and hero—are encapsulated in a critical moment, the Battle of Eichenwalde, which is chronicled in flashback. "We really showcase that life-turning event where his mentor sacrificed himself, which makes Reinhardt believe that a Crusader's job is to shield and protect other people," said director Ben Dai.

"His defining personality trait becomes that he will always rise to a challenge despite all the reasons not to," said senior producer Kevin VanderJagt. "That flashback serves as both a way to give you backstory into the character but also all the context you need to understand why he is making a decision to answer the call in the current time line."

LEFT Final render of Reinhardt honoring his fallen commander, Balderich.

ABOVE Concept of the Overwatch badge Reinhardt lays on the throne where Balderich rests.

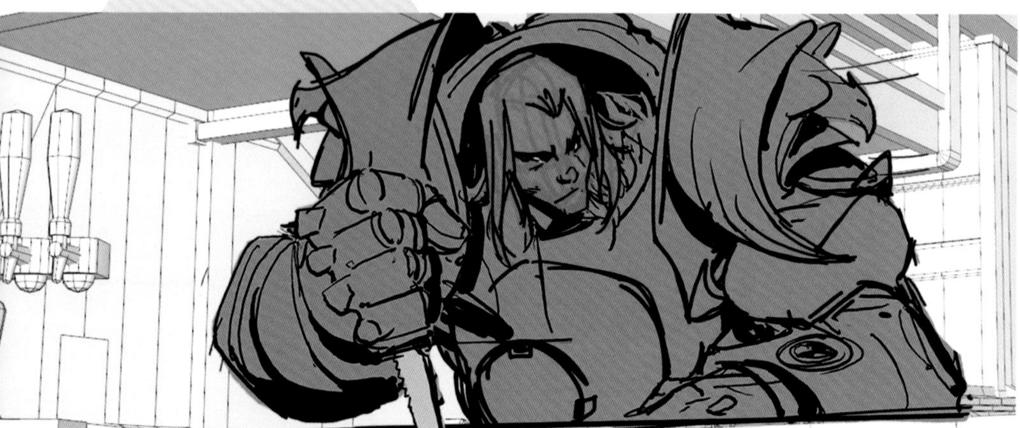

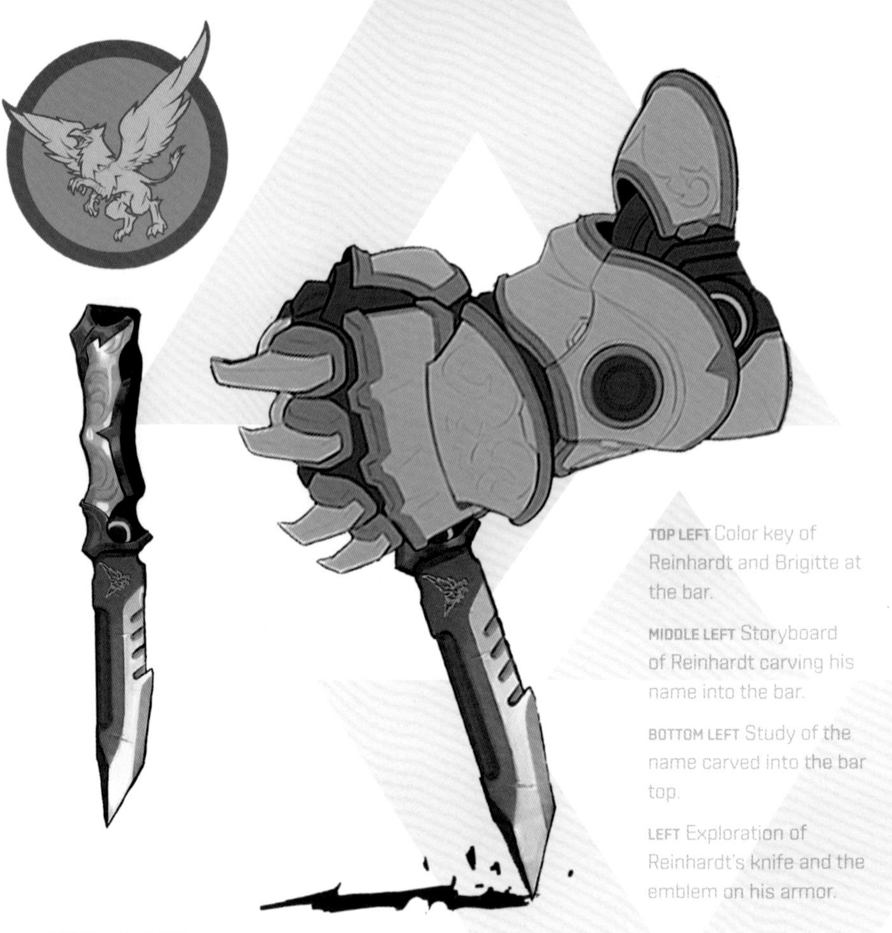

**TOP LEFT** Color key of Reinhardt and Brigitte at the bar.

**MIDDLE LEFT** Storyboard of Reinhardt carving his name into the bar.

**BOTTOM LEFT** Study of the name carved into the bar top.

**LEFT** Exploration of Reinhardt's knife and the emblem on his armor.

## AT THE BAR

Initially, young Reinhardt's motive for joining the battle is glory. He's all ego, even going to the extreme of carving his name into the bar where he raises a toast to battle with his mentor, Balderich, and a couple of German army soldiers.

This moment, which perfectly encapsulates the arrogance of the young warrior, sprang from a detail in the game map, which director of story George Krstic noticed during an early location scouting mission. "I asked our head of lore, Sean Copeland, to fly me through the level to get a view of it that you can't really get when you're playing," said Krstic. "And carved into the bar is Reinhardt's name. I stopped for a second and asked myself, 'What kind of an arrogant person would do that?' And I think that was the question that led us to the piece. We decided to explore that—how at one point Reinhardt was trying to carve his name into the universe. Just that simple detail that an environment designer added triggered all these questions."

"When we learn that a character is from a specific location, we start to think about what we know about that character and how we can inject a little bit of them into the map," said *Overwatch*'s assistant art director Dion Rogers. "A lot of people know that Reinhardt's loud and rambunctious, so we thought he might be the type of guy to carve his name into the bar."

"We always treat Reinhardt's wounded eye as if it's got scar tissue throughout it," said Grant. "For example, the range of motion for the eyebrow is only about 30 percent of that of the other eye. And we never blink the hurt eye. If he blinks, it doesn't close. It just squishes a little bit. We only break that rule when he's going to have his eyes closed for a long period of time."

## REINHARDT'S HAIR

▲ Young Reinhardt is a brash knight who doesn't wear a helmet and who takes pride in his long, flowing blond hair. "From the game's release, he's had this voice line where he says his hair was amazing," said character art director Arnold Tsang. "So that was our launching point—some kind of crazy hair to make him feel like he was super confident, young and fearless."

The hair became so important to the characterization of young Reinhardt that the filmmakers created special simulations to animate it. "We did procedurally generated hair movement," said VFX supervisor Shimon Cohen. "We had three speeds for it—slow, medium, and high. If the wind was really blowing in the shot, we would crank it up." ▼

LEFT Young Reinhardt facial expression studies.

ABOVE Model of young Reinhardt with wounded eye.

## WHAT WOULD REINHARDT DO?

▲ When thinking about how young Reinhardt would enter battle in "Honor and Glory," Dai couldn't help but draw on his own experience playing the character in the game. "I was like, well, he probably just charges right into the line of fire and doesn't really care what the consequences are," said Dai. "And then Jeff Kaplan was like, 'I think that's great because that's what most people who play Reinhardt will respond to, whether they should or should not do it, being a tank.' It's such a temptation! So I was trying to channel that aspect of the gameplay into the movie."

"We have a joke around the office now because of that cinematic," said Rogers. "Every once in a while, you get this Reinhardt player that charges everywhere. So we call that 'Cinematic Reinhardt' because that's how we presented him in the movie. 'Oh, we got a Cinematic Reinhardt on our team!'" ▼

**THESE PAGES** Storyboards depicting key moments from the animated short.

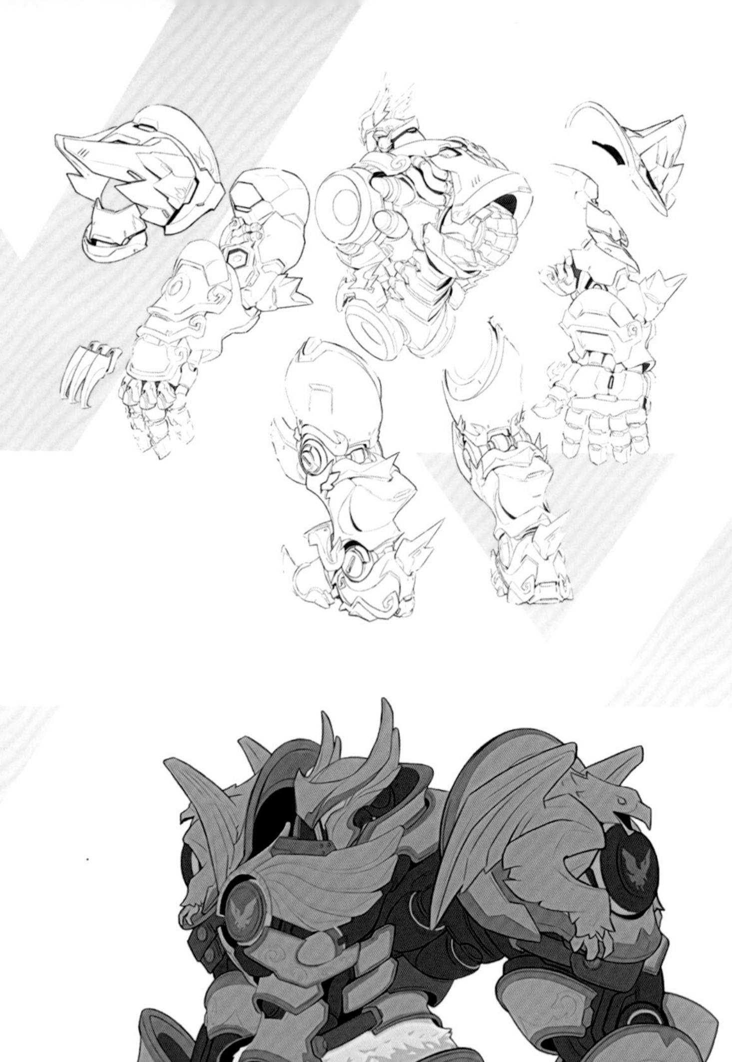

## CRUSADER ARMOR

▲ The Overwatch team wanted to make Balderich's armor feel ornate—like it belonged to a knight from a past era. To do so, they revisited some early character concepts for Reinhardt that had been discarded during initial game development.

"There were some versions of Reinhardt's armor that were more knightly; they had a red cape and everything," said Tsang. "We initially found that was maybe too far. But we thought we'd probably save them for something else down the line. And we ended up using that aesthetic in 'Honor and Glory' for the designs of Balderich and Reinhardt's original armor. We were like, 'Yeah, let's go a little bit more ostentatious and decorative on these guys. These are the glory days, right?'" ▼

**THIS PAGE** Sketch and concepts of elaborate Crusader armor and rocket hammer.

**OPPOSITE** Render of Reinhardt's present-day armor, which is less ornate than the historic Crusader armor.

08

## SLOW MOTION

▲ "Honor and Glory" has a run time of seven and a half minutes, and over a minute of that is in slow motion. "It's life and death," said Dai. "We slowed down time to show Balderich's combat prowess but also to showcase the fact that Reinhardt is really making a change—he's willing to die protecting the soldiers."

Slowing a cinematic down from a customary 24 frames per second to 120 frames per second means that everything must be animated with more detail. "There's really only two ways to do it," said Grant. "One, you animate in real time. Then you can change the settings to be 120 frames a second and tweak and modify the animation as needed. That's the easier way to go about it for consistency. The other way is to animate at 24 frames per second as if it is slow motion. This is harder because you're trying to fake what that frame rate is supposed to look like, and it can be difficult to keep a consistent look across multiple slow-motion shots."

In the case of "Honor and Glory," the Overwatch team chose the easier way, mainly because of the heavy effects work in the slow-motion sequence, which is laden with explosions and gunfire. ▼

**LEFT** Final render of Balderich in combat.

## STREET CLOTHES

▲ "Honor and Glory" is bookended by scenes of Reinhardt and his goddaughter, Brigitte, visiting Eichenwalde in the present, years after the battle that changed the course of Reinhardt's life. This prompted the filmmakers to imagine what the heroes would wear when they aren't girded for battle.

"Jungah Lee did the costumes for both," said Dai. "She did a really cool drawing of Brigitte with a T-shirt that says, 'I work out because I love to eat.' It was perfect.

"I think the artists especially enjoy making up costumes for established characters like Reinhardt. I remember, at one point, we had sort of a biker outfit for him, which changed into more of a tank top and military pants. We have a lot of fun coming up with alternative costumes, and some of them eventually become skins you can use in the game." ▼

**TOP LEFT** Concept of a shirtless, wounded Reinhardt.

**LEFT** Costume exploration for present-day Reinhardt.

**ABOVE & OPPOSITE, BOTTOM** Costume explorations for Brigitte.

**OPPOSITE, TOP** Brigitte facial expression studies.

## HONORING EICHENWALDE

The environment artists try to imbue a map with lore throughout the level design process. This practice was especially important in the case of Eichenwalde, which was the site of an important battle during the Omnic Crisis. In the game, the map exhibits the aftereffects of the conflict. But most of "Honor and Glory" takes place before and during the battle, which gave the artists an opportunity to imagine what the city would have looked like as it prepared for the coming omnic invasion.

"We wanted to depict what happened to this place before it became a battleground: What would the inhabitants have done knowing that an imminent attack was on the way," said Rogers. "So there's some signage in German that speaks to leaving the area. And the Crusader posters reinforce the idea that there was this group of people that would help. And then obviously Balderich's armor. We didn't know a lot about him at first; we just heard that he had died in Eichenwalde Castle. We imagined they took him away but left the armor."

For the cinematic, the team adopted what the environment artists had created and sought to explain why that suit of armor was on the throne—and why it matters so much. "We wanted to embrace the game mechanics. To explore that detail. To explain it and weave it into the story so it's more of a holistic experience, rather than the game is the game and the story is the story. We try to make it as unified as possible," said Krstic.

**RIGHT** Color key of Reinhardt and Brigitte's van arriving in Eichenwalde.

BRAUEREI
ACHTUNG
MINEN

The two soldiers who are sitting at the bar at the beginning of the film are the same ones that Reinhardt shields at the end. They are also modeled after two Blizzard employees—Shimon Cohen, who worked as VFX supervisor on the piece, and Steeg Haskell, the rigging and simulation supervisor.

**THESE PAGES** Concepts of two soldiers who appear multiple times in the animated short.

SAFTY PIN
U28 001

## AT WAR

If one were to place "Honor and Glory" in a cinematic genre, it would clearly be a war movie, a point of reference that the filmmakers consciously embraced as they pushed the Overwatch aesthetic in new directions for the piece. "There are two distinct moods in this show—a contrast between the warm, late-afternoon, nostalgic vibe of the present day that we see at the beginning and end of the show, and the desaturated brutal flashback sequence that comprises most of the shots, which feel like a grim war movie where explosions and other effects stand out," said former art director Mathias Verhasselt.

Compared to other prerendered cinematics, the battle sequence in "Honor and Glory" has a muted color palette, and its lighting and effects are more realistic. These features run counter to Overwatch's general look, but they make perfect sense in the context of Reinhardt's memory of the battle.

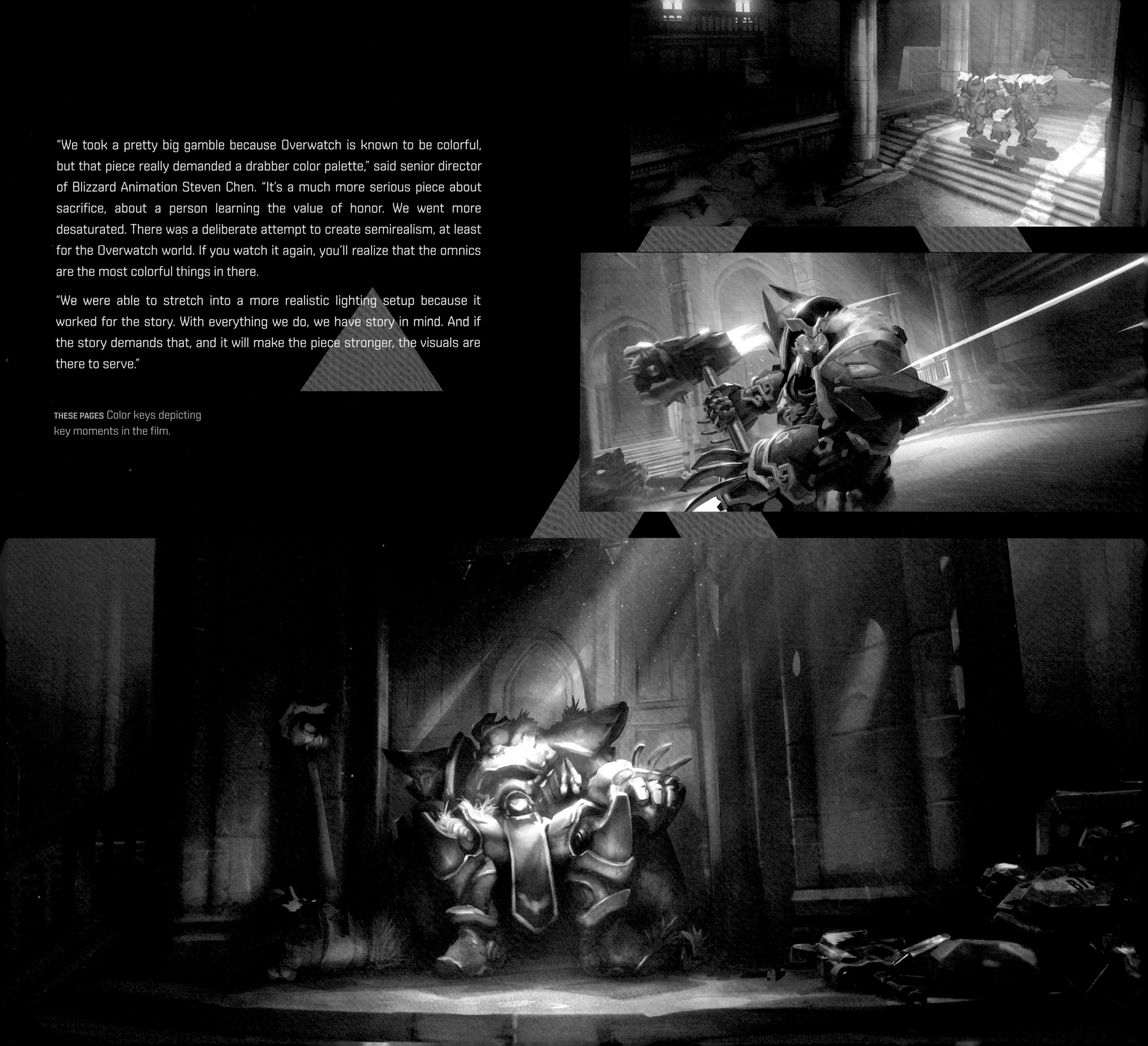

"We took a pretty big gamble because Overwatch is known to be colorful, but that piece really demanded a drabber color palette," said senior director of Blizzard Animation Steven Chen. "It's a much more serious piece about sacrifice, about a person learning the value of honor. We went more desaturated. There was a deliberate attempt to create semirealism, at least for the Overwatch world. If you watch it again, you'll realize that the omnics are the most colorful things in there.

"We were able to stretch into a more realistic lighting setup because it worked for the story. With everything we do, we have story in mind. And if the story demands that, and it will make the piece stronger, the visuals are there to serve."

**THESE PAGES** Color keys depicting key moments in the film.

**RIGHT** Final render of Reinhardt from the end of the animated short.

# SHOOTING STAR

"THE REST OF THE SQUAD, THE COUNTRY, THEY'RE ALL COUNTING ON ME."

—D.VA

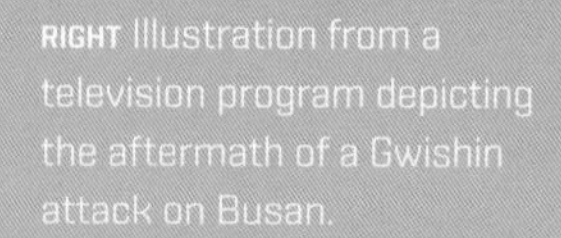

**RIGHT** Illustration from a television program depicting the aftermath of a Gwishin attack on Busan.

노래연습장
노래방
출입금지

**FAR LEFT & OPPOSITE** Costume explorations for D.Va.

**LEFT** Concept of food packaging featuring the celebrity D.Va.

**"SHOOTING STAR"—RELEASED ON AUGUST 22, 2018—IS THE** only animated short in the second wave of cinematics that doesn't tie in to the reunification of Overwatch. "The initial instinct was to make D.Va's episode about how she's connected to the recall message," said senior producer Kevin VanderJagt. "But every time we tried to figure out a thread for how we would get there, it just felt forced. At the end of the day, she has no Overwatch affiliation going into the game. She's a young hotshot pilot for a military organization in Korea and a defender of her people, but she's not on that global stage yet."

Having made the decision to forego tying in with "Recall," the Overwatch team put a greater focus on D.Va herself—not as she appears publicly but in her private life. "We tried to figure out what she would do on her day off," said director Ben Dai.

"In game, she had been portrayed as this kind of rock star. She's a pro gamer," said senior writer Matt Burns. "We wanted to show her behind the scenes, contrasting when she's on the news and in the spotlight with her in the mech hangar covered in grease."

"Even just that little detail of the grease smear on her cheek, as opposed to the triangular makeup that she wears when she's presenting herself in public, was very intentional," said VanderJagt. "And she literally lets her hair down, which makes her feel like a more real and relatable character."

NANO
COLA
NANO
NANO
COLA
NANO
COLA
NANO
COLA

THIS PAGE Color keys depicting key moments in the film.

Crucial to this idea of making D.Va seem more approachable was the foil of Dae-hyun, D.Va's mechanic and friend who has supported her since early in her career. "We wanted to have a character who knew the real D.Va, like he's with her when she's not in front of the camera," said Burns. "He's someone who knows what she's actually going through, even if she doesn't vocalize it, and someone who can speak truth to her."

Originally, Dae-hyun was going to be more of a bystander who stayed in the base and gave D.Va advice while she battled the Gwishin. But that kept Dae-hyun in a subordinate position, both professionally and personally. The filmmakers wanted to give Dae-hyun a more active role that would bring him and D.Va closer together and establish a less hierarchical relationship between them. Eventually, the filmmakers decided that Dae-hyun would overload the mech's reactor from afar, helping D.Va turn her mech into a bomb to defeat the final enemy Gwishin and save the city of Busan.

Showing the more personal side of how D.Va and Dae-hyun relate to each other was challenging for the animators, who had to figure out how D.Va, who is normally so composed in public, could subtly navigate the nuances of their relationship.

"The funny thing about 'Shooting Star' is that all the shots that we were the most worried about—all the mech sequences with the giant tentacles and fighting—were relatively easy," said animation supervisor Hunter Grant. "What we should have been worried about were the sequences of D.Va in the hangar."

**FAR LEFT & TOP RIGHT** Concepts of Dae-hyun.

**LEFT** Dae-hyun facial expression studies.

**OPPOSITE** D.Va facial expression studies.

**OPPOSITE, BOTTOM RIGHT** Concept of D.Va featuring her MEKA jacket.

MEKA

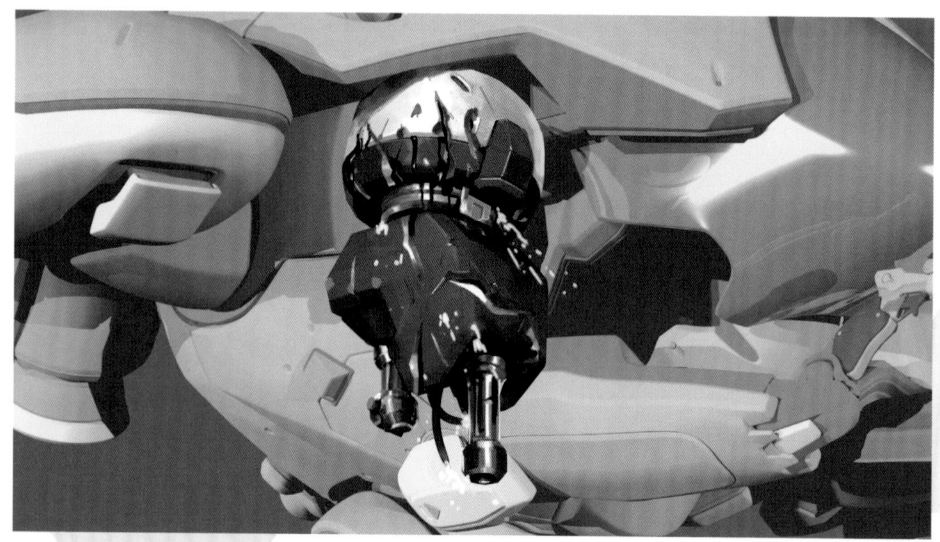

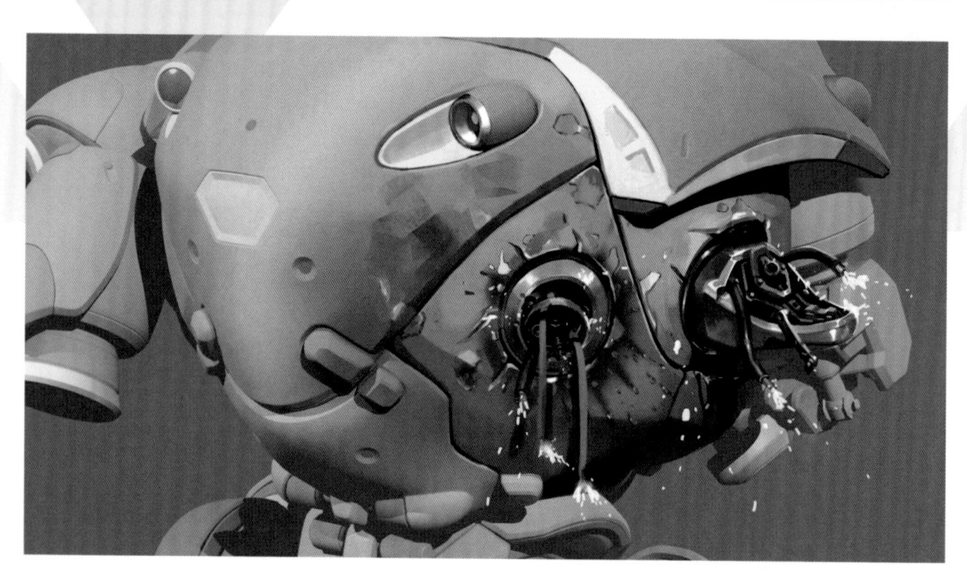

**LEFT** Explorations of the damage suffered by D.Va's mech.

**ABOVE & OPPOSITE** Concepts exploring D.Va's injuries and her costuming during her recovery.

디바짱♥
디아블로 부터
나는커서 누나처럼 될거에요
사랑해
사랑까지 너프할순없어!
나두♥
화이팅!!
푹 쉬어요, 디바!
고마워요
영원히 팬♥
송하나 내꼬
부산 병원
디바짱
고마워요
송하나 내꼬
사랑해
나두♥

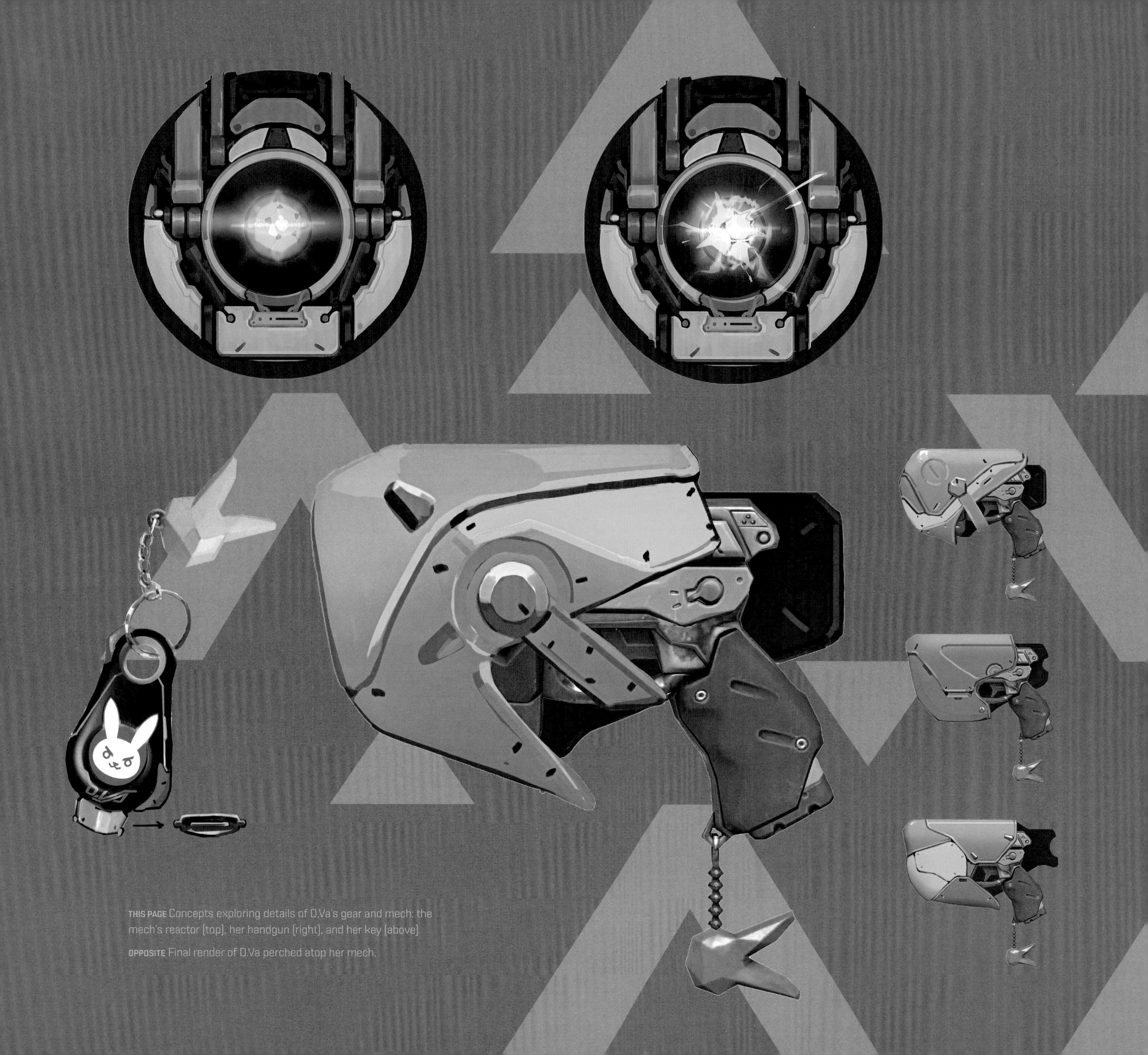


**THIS PAGE** Concepts exploring details of D.Va's gear and mech: the mech's reactor (top), her handgun (right), and her key (above).

**OPPOSITE** Final render of D.Va perched atop her mech.

### CHANGE OF MISSION

▲ In early discussions, before the decision was made to separate "Shooting Star" from the overarching "Recall" story, the Overwatch team explored a wide range of ideas, some of which were eventually incorporated into the *Overwatch 2* announcement trailer.

"The initial idea for 'Shooting Star' was to have D.Va fight against a giant mech," said VanderJagt. "At the end of the day, we decided on an aerial dogfight, but the giant mech was something we still really wanted to do. So we went back to it for 'Zero Hour.' Very rarely do we develop an idea that we really like and just leave it on the table. Usually, if there's something cool that we come up with, we'll try and find a way to work it into another story."

In the original idea, D.Va's confrontation with the giant mech, which was to rise from the ocean like a kaiju, was going to end on a cliffhanger. The reformed Overwatch would then arrive in the second part of the story to help her save Busan, much like they do for Paris in "Zero Hour."

"One of the main reasons we didn't goes back to making this story all about D.Va," said Burns. "We wanted to see her rise to the challenge and overcome the obstacles—both physical and emotional—that she's wrestling with. If Overwatch had come in and defeated the mech, that would have stolen an important moment of character growth from D.Va." ▼

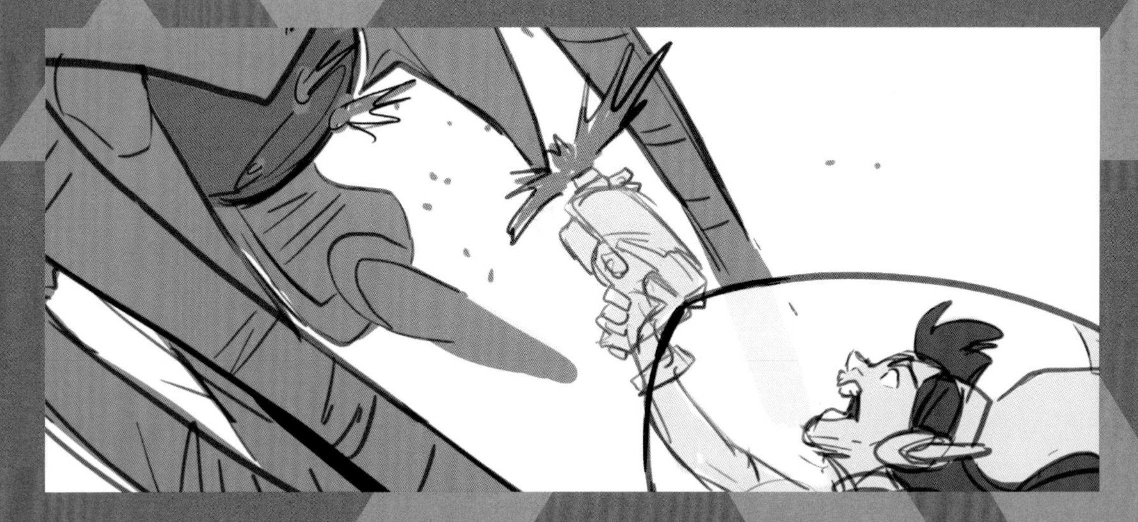

**THESE PAGES** Storyboards of D.Va's battle with the Gwishin.

## GREATER STAKES

The decision to focus on character and dispense with a tie-in to "Recall" allowed the Overwatch team to plant seeds for future stories about another area of conflict: South Korea, and the deadly Gwishin omnics that attack the country on a periodic basis.

"We said, 'We're still setting the stage because we know D.Va's an important character, and we know she's going to be part of the narrative once Overwatch reforms; she's just not there yet,'" said VanderJagt. "So exploring where she is and who she is was still really relevant to the overall story, even though it doesn't directly tie in to the 'Recall' narrative. It at least established her character in terms of where she is, what the status of the MEKA squad is, and the struggles that they're still facing. In a lot of ways, they're still fighting remnants of the enemy that Overwatch faced during the Omnic Crisis years ago."

"In terms of world building, we wanted to show that in Korea, there's a unique situation where there's this offshore base of enemy omnics," said Burns. "That's why D.Va and the MEKA squad exist—to defend Busan from recurring attacks. We wanted to fill out the world and show that some places like Numbani are generally peaceful, and then there are places like Russia or Korea, plagued by constant conflict.

"It's a reminder that the Overwatch world is still a dangerous place. Even though there is hope for a better world, things have not been going well. There are these threats that exist. And that's why heroes like D.Va, the MEKA squad, and Overwatch are needed."

"Shooting Star" begins with an aerial shot of Busan, which is a detailed and dynamic matte painting, rather than a fully modeled 3D environment. "It was originally just supposed to be a painting that we were going to cut into and cut out of," said visual effects art director Anthony Eftekhari. "But we thought it'd be really cool if we could move the camera through the city. So we populated it with streetlights and cars and trains and all sorts of things to give it life. Matte painting has evolved to provide a lot of the visual direction on some of the environments and taken on a much larger role as the shows have progressed."

**RIGHT** Final render of the MEKA base with Busan in the background in daylight.

부
산

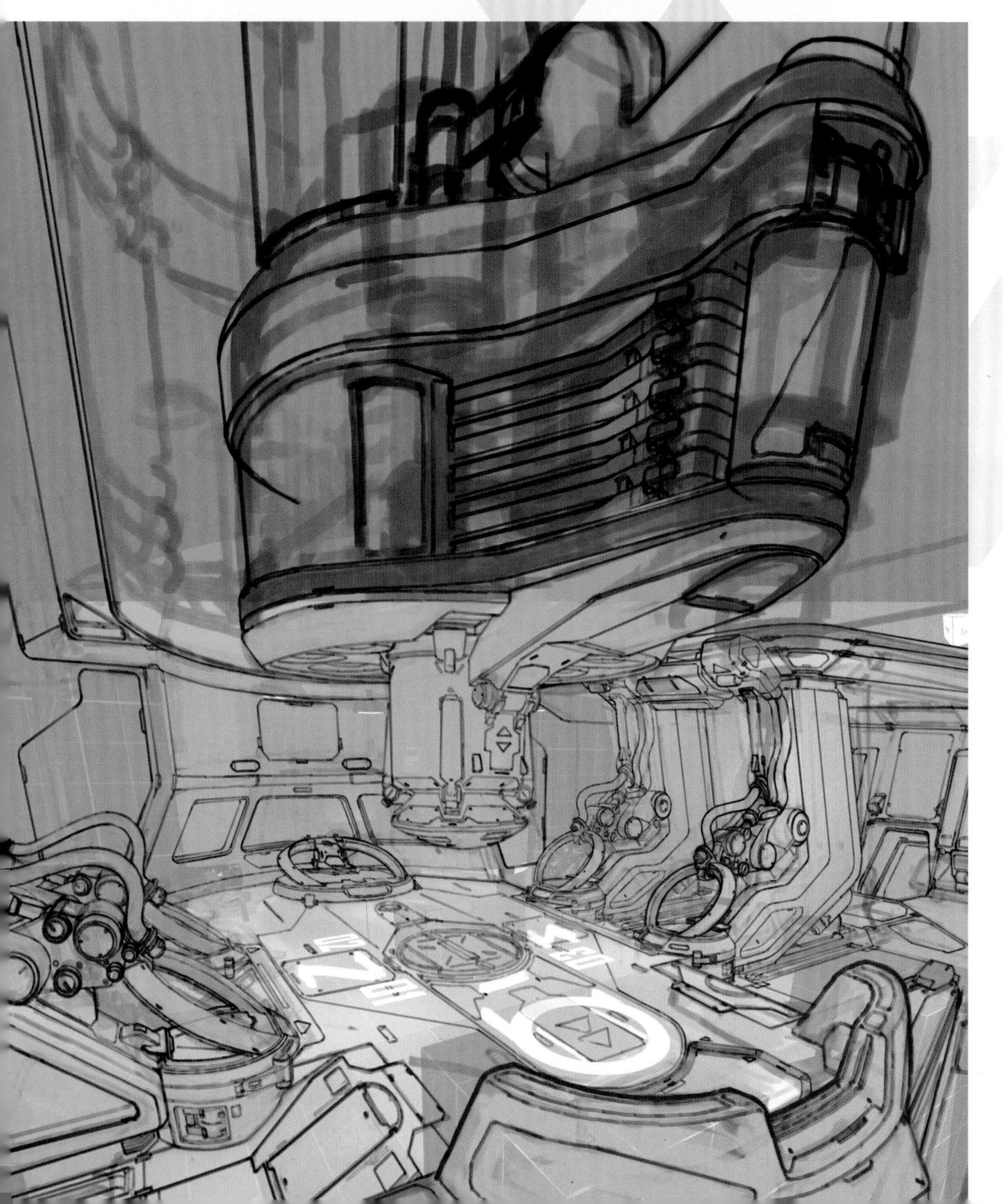

## THE MEKA BASE

▲ Previous prerendered cinematics had been staged on game maps that already existed or which were nearly finished. This allowed the Overwatch team to scout the locations and decide where the films would take place. With "Shooting Star," though, the filmmakers didn't have that luxury. The Busan map was just starting development when production on the cinematic began, and both the animated short and the game level were timed for the Korean Overwatch Fan Festival in August 2018.

To accommodate this unique situation, the artists working on the cinematic volunteered to finalize the design for the MEKA base, the in-game location where most of the film would take place. "We had most of the general building blocks for the map," said Dai. "So we drew our concepts over the rough geometry. We knew the basics, like where a door had to be because of gameplay reasons, or if there was a pillar to block line of sight."

"It was like a reverse approach this time, where the cinematic modelers gave us a ton of the pieces to start," said *Overwatch*'s assistant art director Dion Rogers. "We took their files and used them to help start the game version of the map. So what's in game is basically what you see in the cinematic." ▼

**TOP LEFT** Concept of the MEKA base with Busan in the background.

**LEFT, BELOW & OPPOSITE** Concepts of different areas inside the MEKA base.

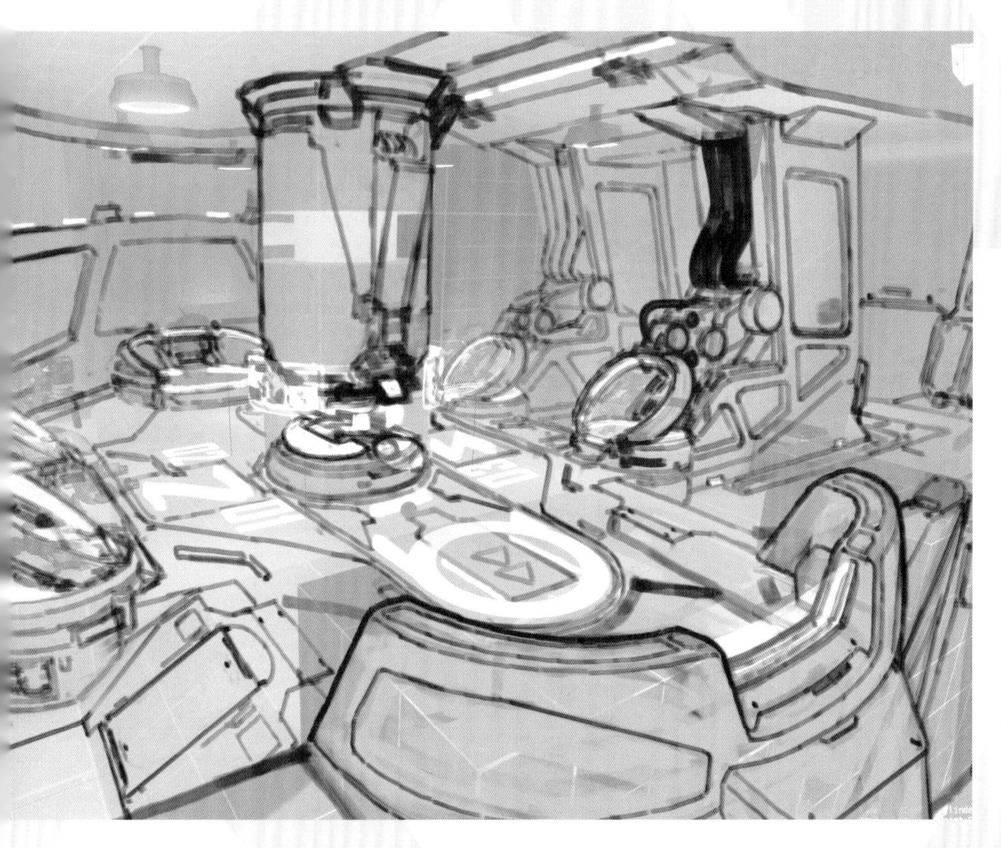

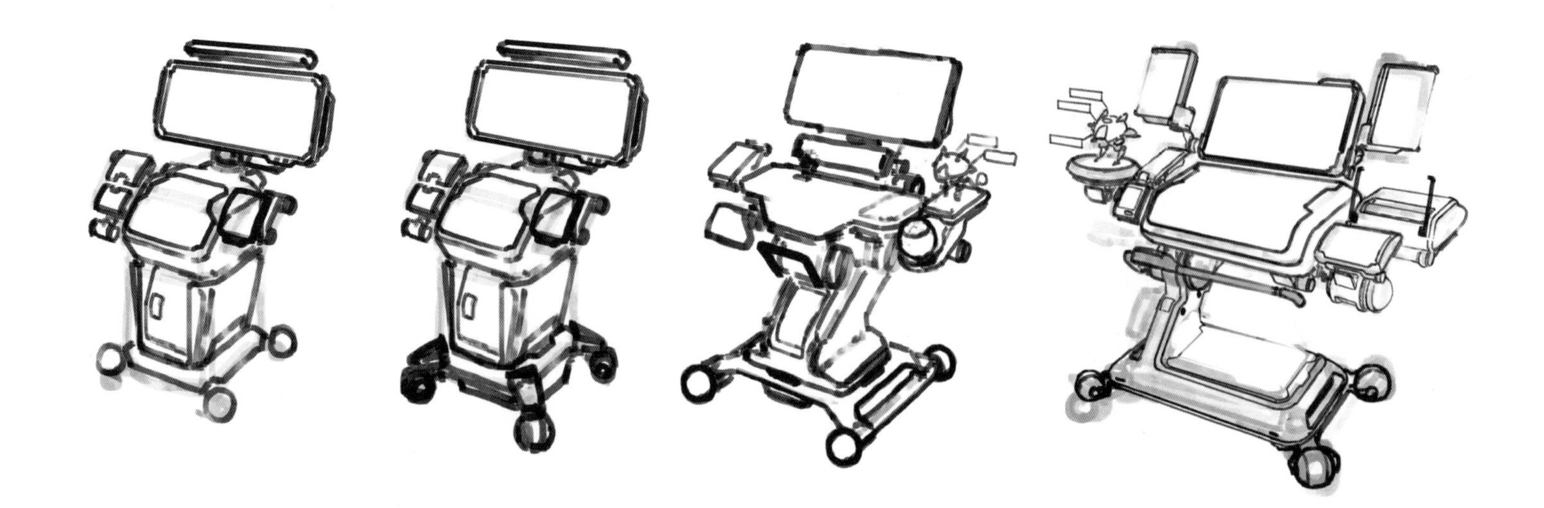

**THESE PAGES** Concepts of Dae-hyun's workstation.

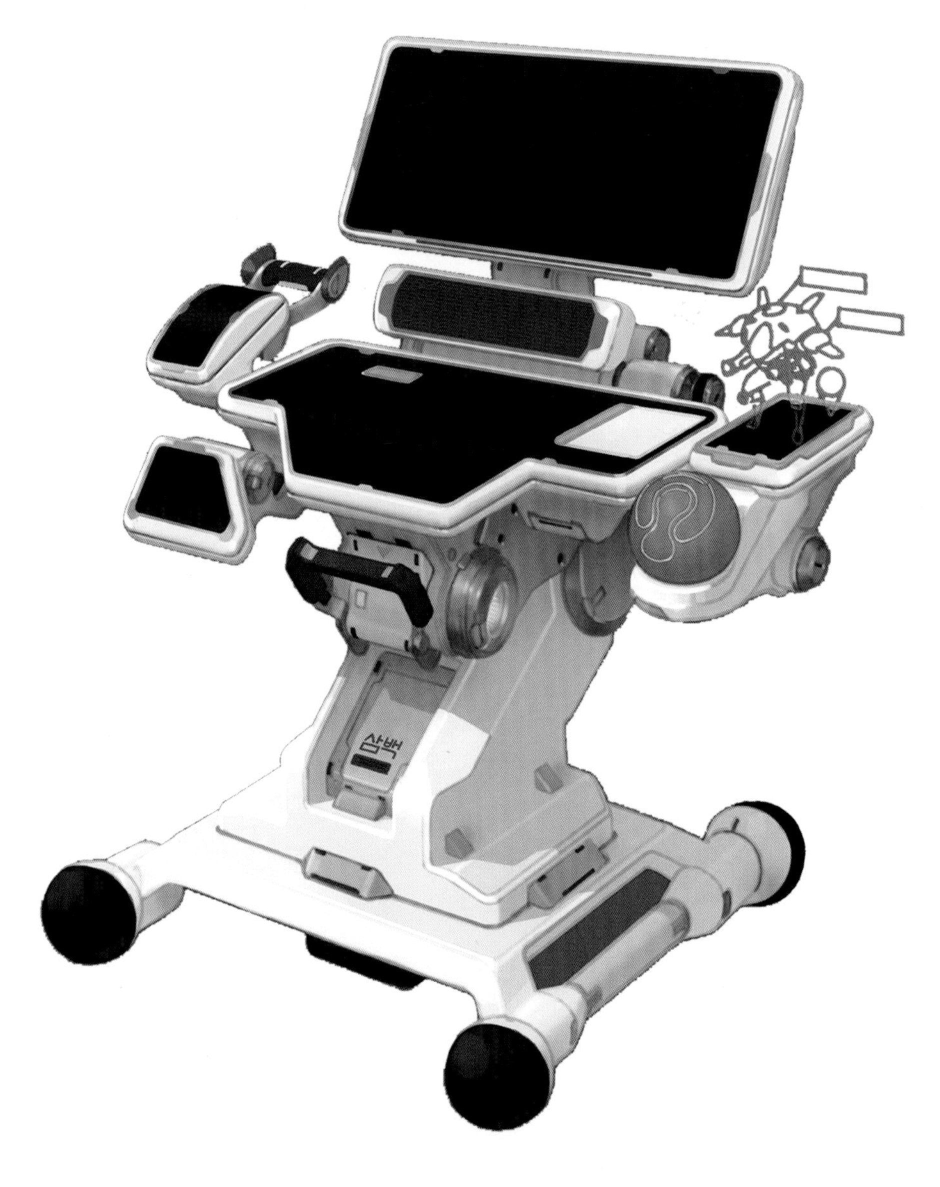

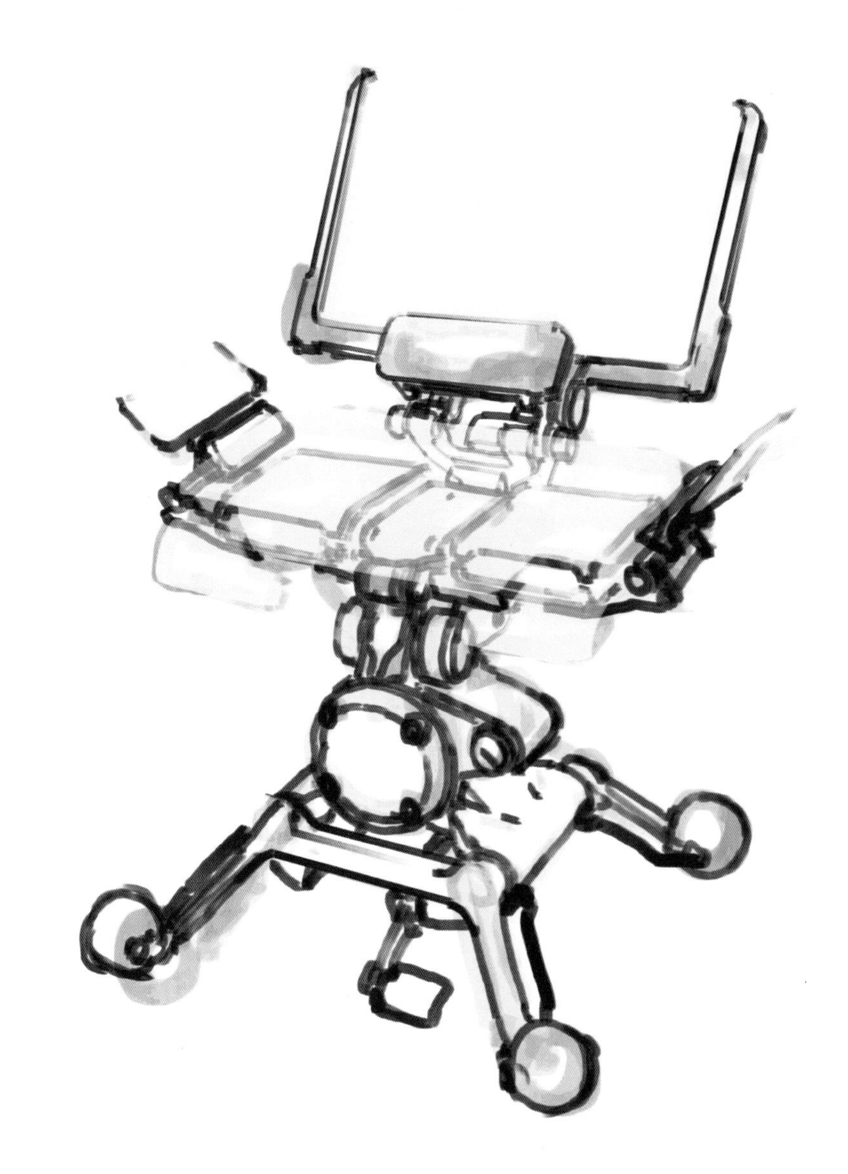

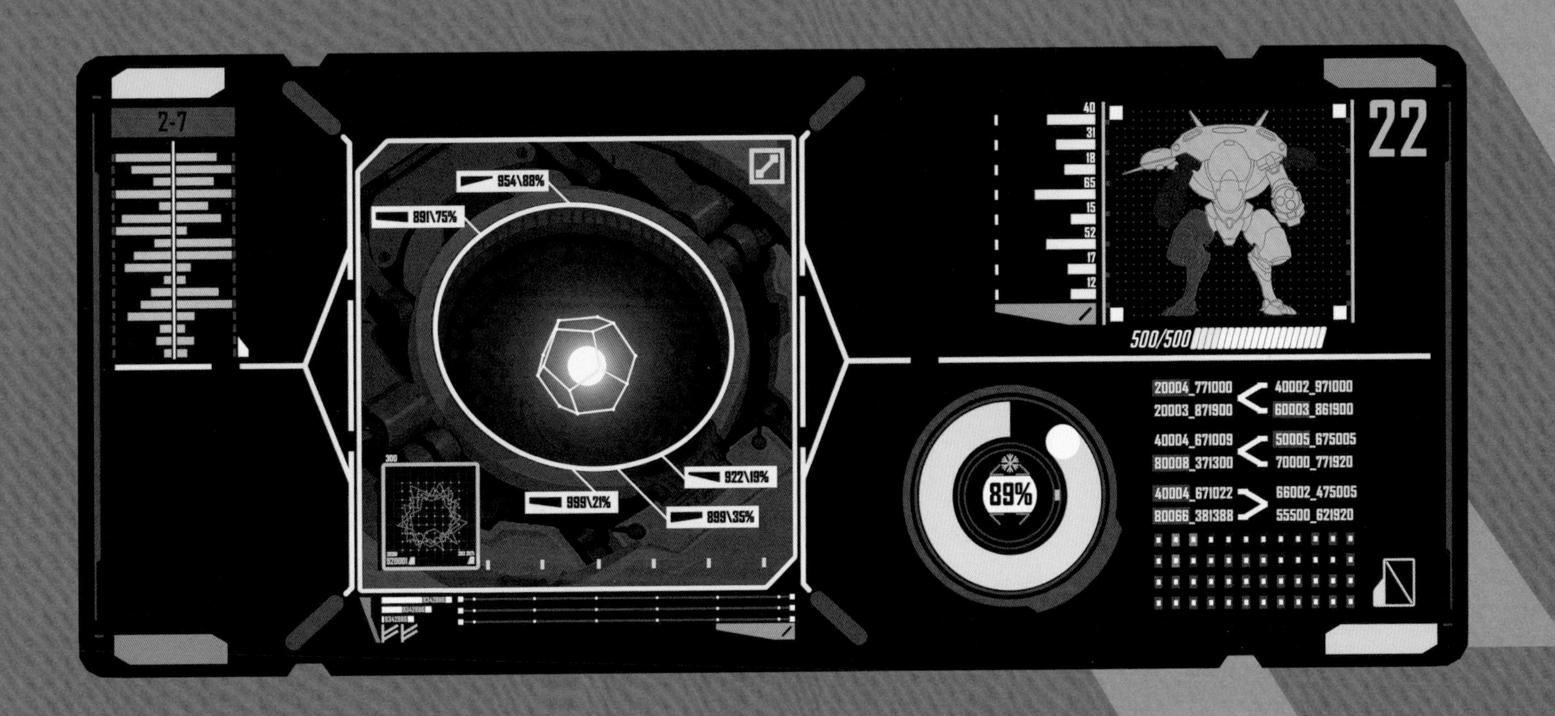
2-7
954\88%
891\75%
922\19%
999\21%
899\35%
22
500/500
89%
20004_771000
20003_871900
40002_971000
60003_861900
40004_671009
80008_371300
50005_675005
70000_771920
40004_671022
80066_381388
66002_475005
55500_621920

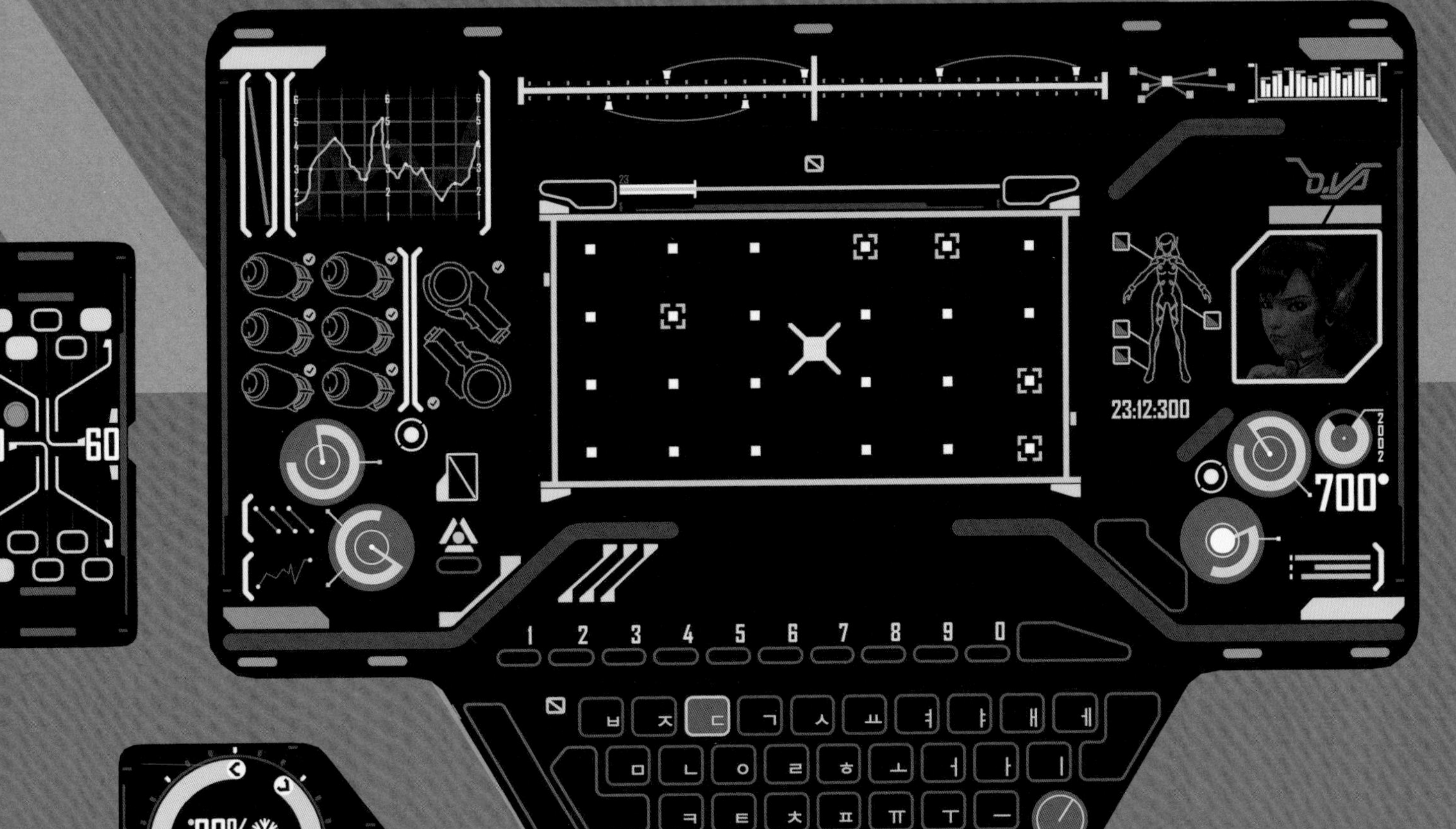
D.VA
23:12:300
700
1 2 3 4 5 6 7 8 9 0
ㅂ ㅈ ㄷ ㄱ ㅅ ㅛ ㅕ ㅑ ㅐ ㅔ
ㅁ ㄴ ㅇ ㄹ ㅎ ㅗ ㅓ ㅏ ㅣ
ㅋ ㅌ ㅊ ㅍ ㅠ ㅜ ㅡ

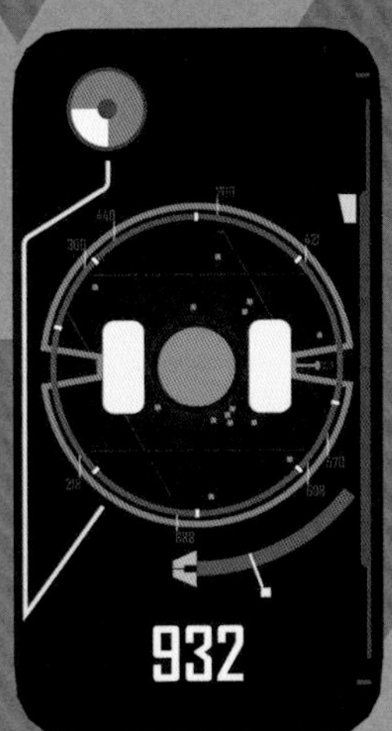
932

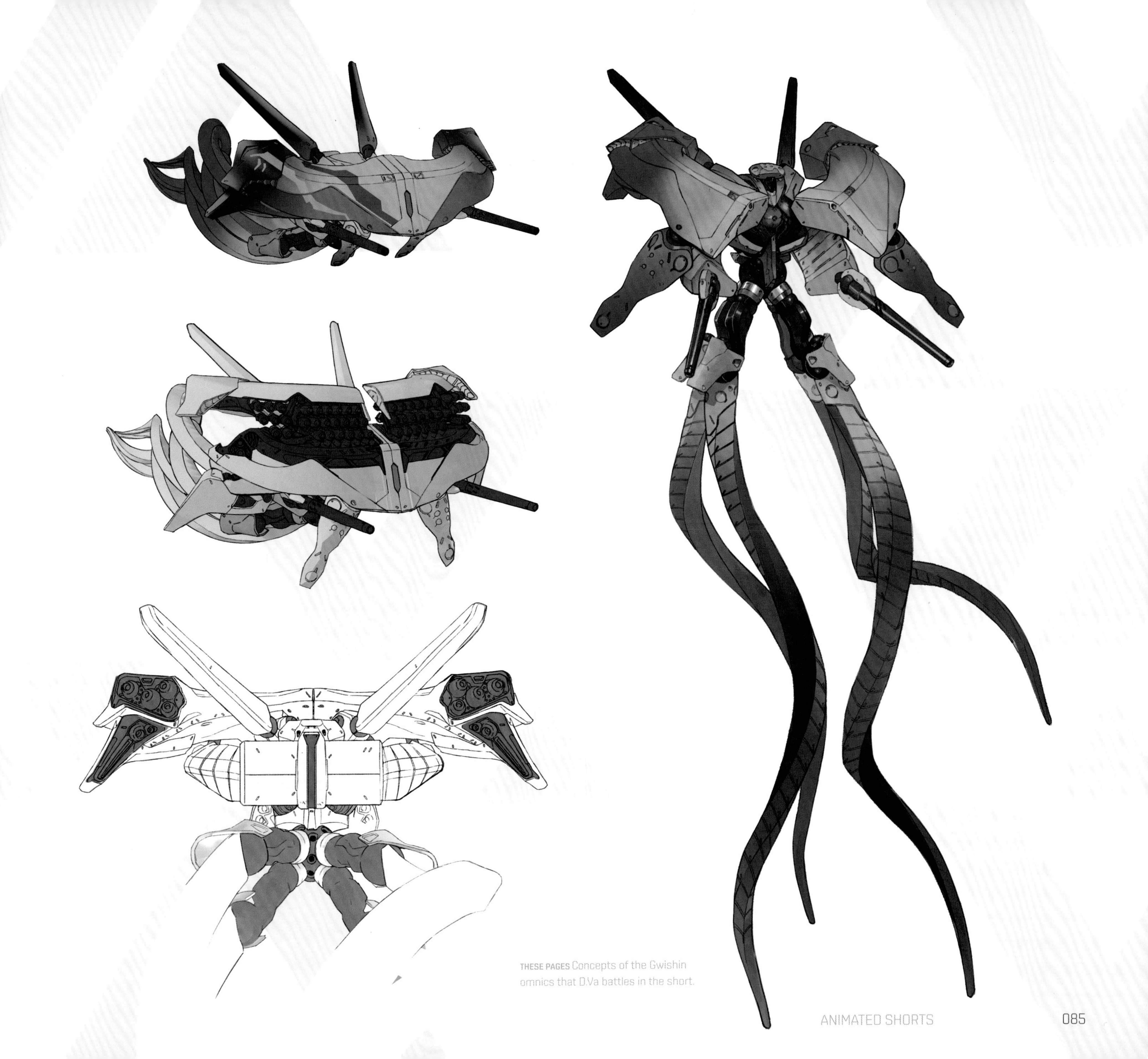

**THESE PAGES** Concepts of the Gwishin omnics that D.Va battles in the short.

## OVER SEA

▲ The dogfight between D.Va and the Gwishin is fast, and it covers a large distance. To make this work, the filmmakers had to build out a suitably vast virtual space that could serve as the set for the cinematic's action sequences.

"We had an actual miles-per-hour gauge that we made to show us how much distance D.Va and the Gwishin cover and how quickly they cover it," said VFX supervisor Shimon Cohen. "And we found it was an enormous distance in 3D, which is something we hadn't really thought about before since most of our shorts take place within sets that are smaller than a football field. This was easily a square mile. So what we did was create three visual layers: where the action was taking place, which was high resolution; and then another that was all procedurally generated; and then ultimately, as you get to the far back, a matte painting." ▼

**THESE PAGES** Color keys of pivotal moments in the film's battle sequence.

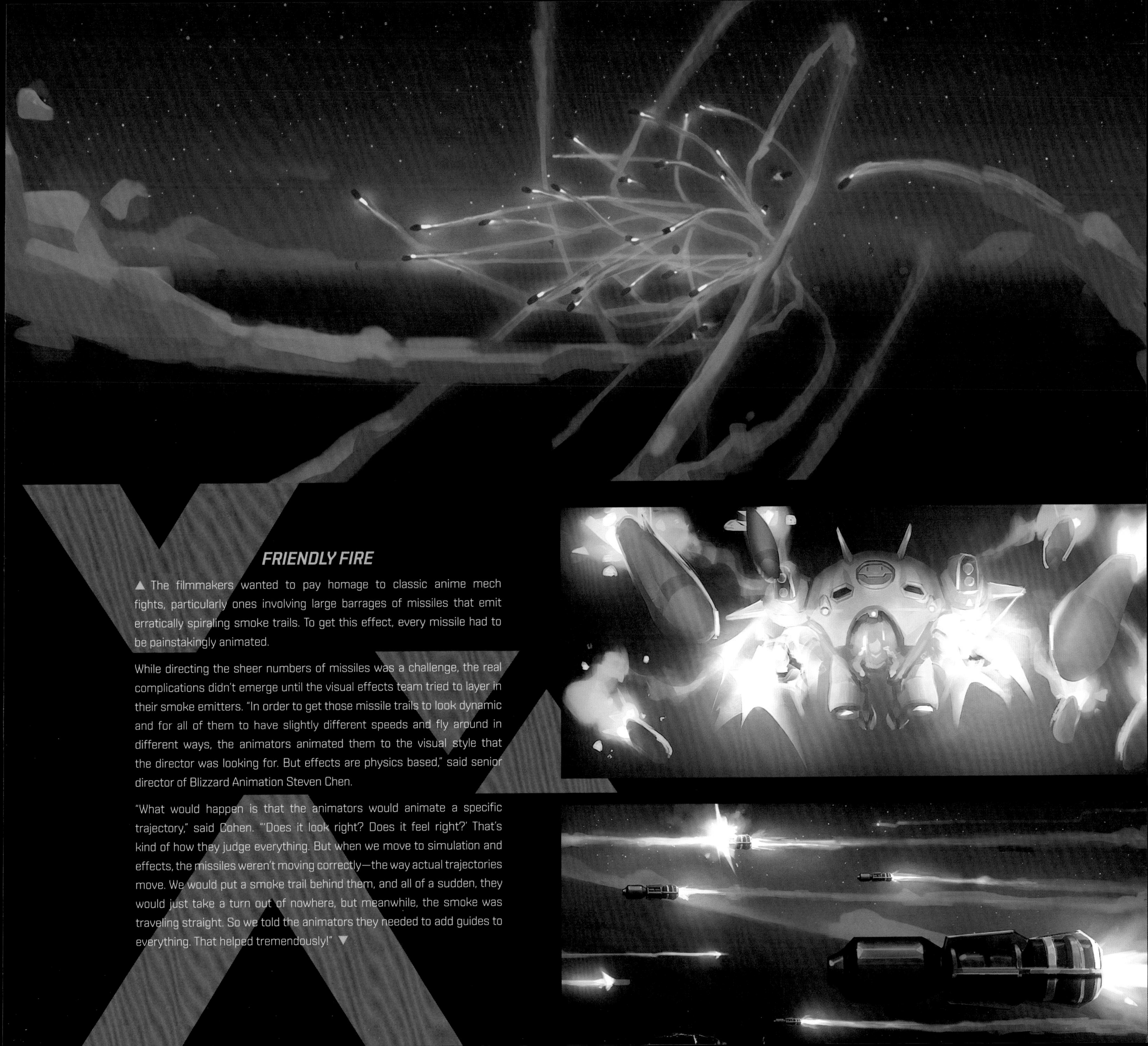

## FRIENDLY FIRE

▲ The filmmakers wanted to pay homage to classic anime mech fights, particularly ones involving large barrages of missiles that emit erratically spiraling smoke trails. To get this effect, every missile had to be painstakingly animated.

While directing the sheer numbers of missiles was a challenge, the real complications didn't emerge until the visual effects team tried to layer in their smoke emitters. "In order to get those missile trails to look dynamic and for all of them to have slightly different speeds and fly around in different ways, the animators animated them to the visual style that the director was looking for. But effects are physics based," said senior director of Blizzard Animation Steven Chen.

"What would happen is that the animators would animate a specific trajectory," said Cohen. "'Does it look right? Does it feel right?' That's kind of how they judge everything. But when we move to simulation and effects, the missiles weren't moving correctly—the way actual trajectories move. We would put a smoke trail behind them, and all of a sudden, they would just take a turn out of nowhere, but meanwhile, the smoke was traveling straight. So we told the animators they needed to add guides to everything. That helped tremendously!" ▼

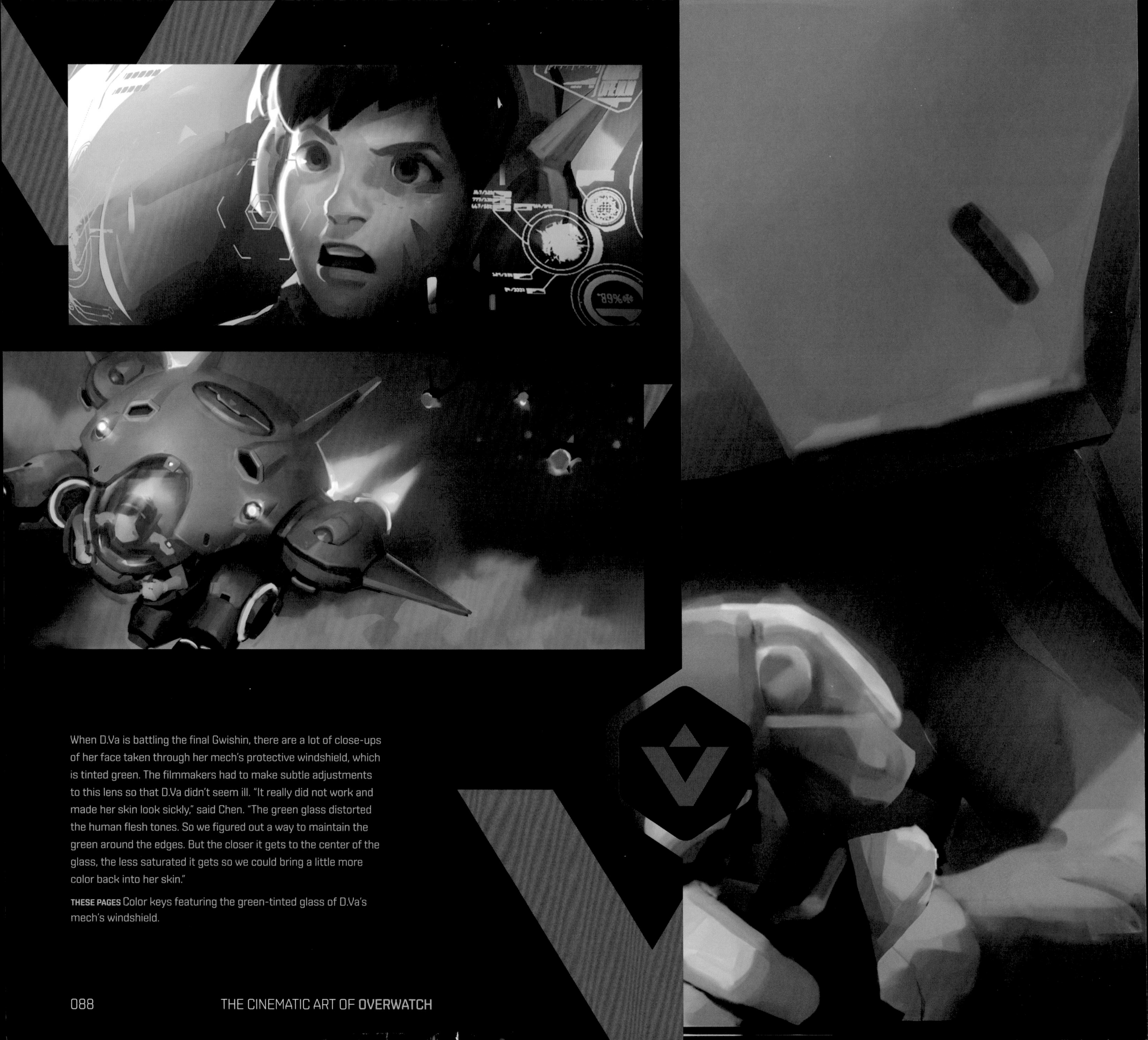

When D.Va is battling the final Gwishin, there are a lot of close-ups of her face taken through her mech's protective windshield, which is tinted green. The filmmakers had to make subtle adjustments to this lens so that D.Va didn't seem ill. "It really did not work and made her skin look sickly," said Chen. "The green glass distorted the human flesh tones. So we figured out a way to maintain the green around the edges. But the closer it gets to the center of the glass, the less saturated it gets so we could bring a little more color back into her skin."

**THESE PAGES** Color keys featuring the green-tinted glass of D.Va's mech's windshield.

**THESE PAGES** Color keys of pivotal moments in the film's battle sequence.

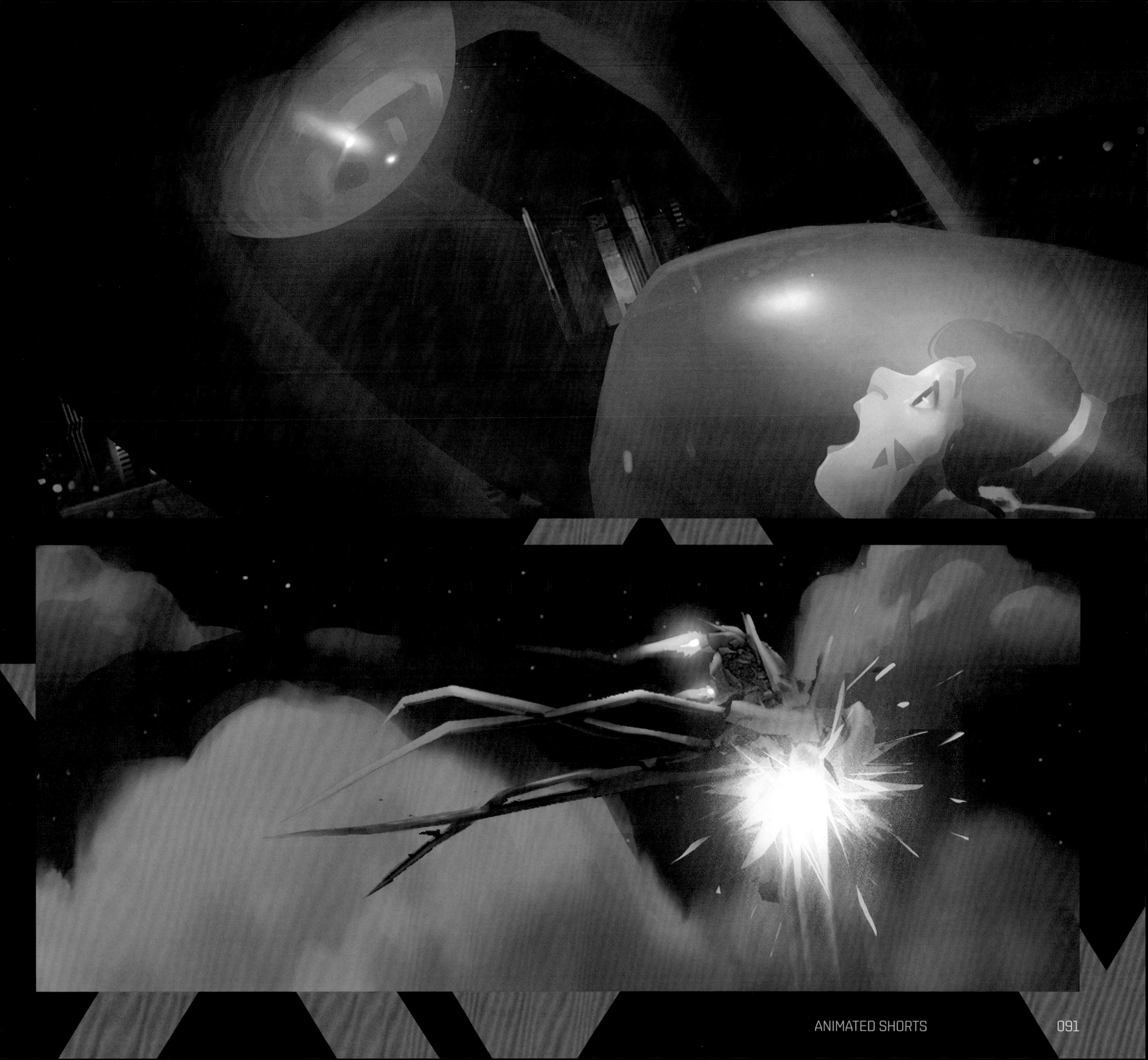

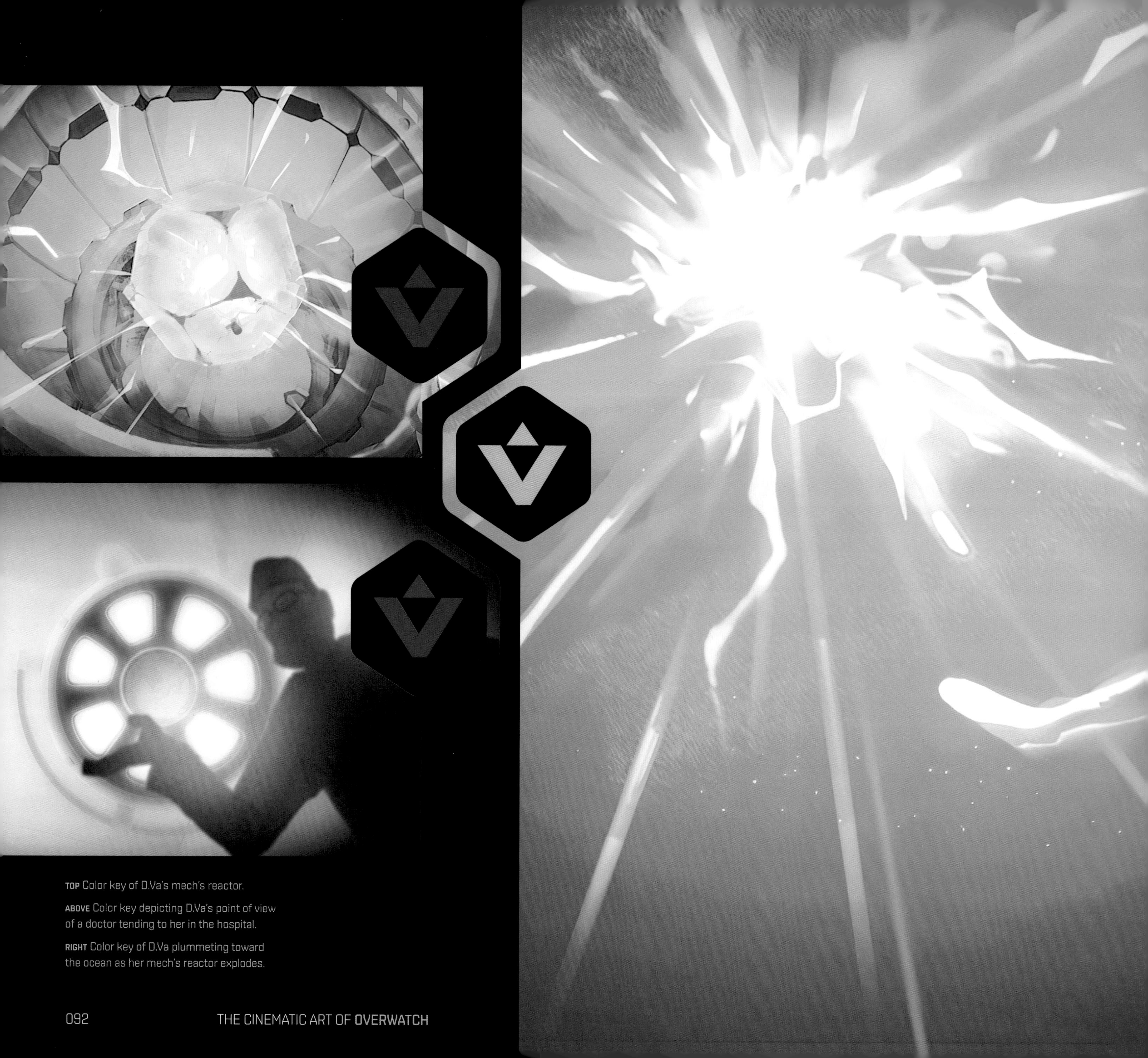

**TOP** Color key of D.Va's mech's reactor.

**ABOVE** Color key depicting D.Va's point of view of a doctor tending to her in the hospital.

**RIGHT** Color key of D.Va plummeting toward the ocean as her mech's reactor explodes.

# REUNION

"JESSE MCCREE. BEEN A WHILE. YOU PROMISED YOU'D WRITE."

—ASHE

**RIGHT** Color key from the short featuring McCree, B.O.B., and Ashe.

**WITH "REUNION," RELEASED NOVEMBER 2, 2018, AT BLIZZCON,** the Overwatch team used lessons learned from the success of "Honor and Glory" and adapted another tried and true cinematic genre: the Western. It was time, though, after the gut-wrenching experiences of "Rise and Shine" and "Honor and Glory," to approach storytelling with a lighter touch.

"This was a palate cleanser," said director of story George Krstic. "We had just done some emotionally taxing pieces and saw the opportunity to have fun with one. There are tiny bits of humor embedded that are inescapable, and you don't come away feeling drained; you come away feeling reenergized."

To find the right tone, the team drew inspiration from some of the more self-conscious entries in the genre, the Italian Westerns of the 1960s and 1970s. "It just flowed from there," said Krstic. "We talked about the things we love about those films. The long holds, the stillness, the quiet, the tension."

This emphasis on achieving the right atmosphere allowed the filmmakers to explore various plot ideas. "The initial pitch for the story was, 'Hey, guys, let's not do anything complicated. Let's just do a spaghetti Western,'" said senior producer Kevin VanderJagt. "But it's Blizzard. So we can't just do a spaghetti Western; we can't just do a straight shot. We ended up realizing that there was an opportunity to inject some really meaningful backstory in a subtle way."

Director Jason Hill also wanted to make sure that "Reunion" was character driven, rather than solely about action and exposition. "I wanted to make a smaller, more personal piece," said Hill. "So the Deadlock Gang—McCree's adversaries—became more interesting to me than anything else because we hadn't explored them yet. And I was like, 'We need somebody to run this gang, somebody who is as cool as McCree.'"

LEFT Concept of the jukebox in the diner at the beginning of the animated short.

ABOVE Concept of the record that plays in the jukebox during the film's title sequence.

OPPOSITE, TOP Concept of Ashe's keepsake photograph taken when she and McCree were both part of the Deadlock Gang.

OPPOSITE, BOTTOM Concept of Ashe on her hoverbike.

OPPOSITE, FAR RIGHT Explorations of Ashe's keychain.

The filmmakers wanted to add a photo to the film that alluded to McCree and Ashe's history together. At first, it was going to appear at the beginning in the diner scene, but they decided to make it one of Ashe's keepsakes, attaching it to her hoverbike. Visual development artist Jungah Lee set the image at the Deadlock Gang's hideout in the Route 66 map, making McCree's reunion with Ashe and the rest of the gang all the more poignant.

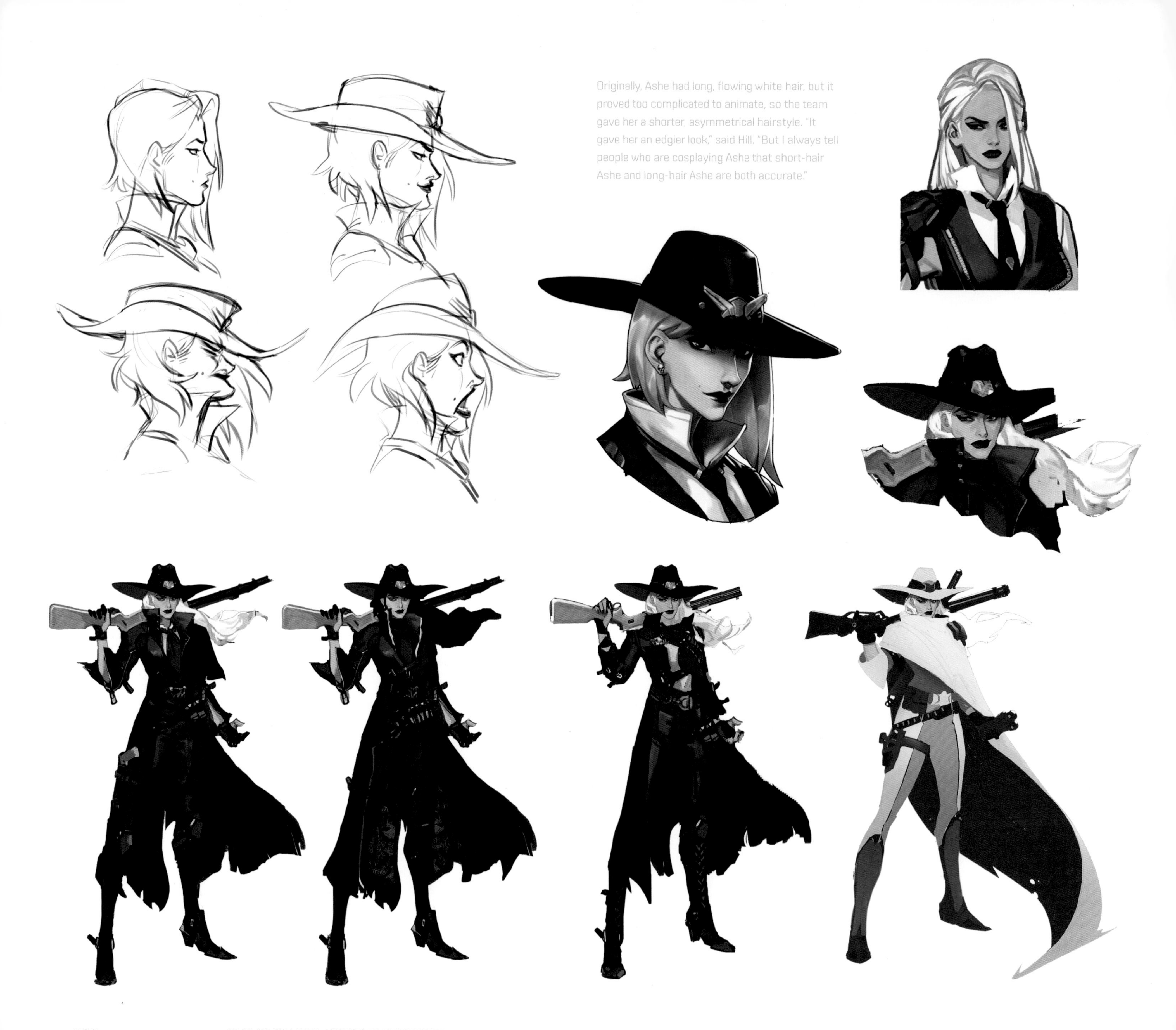

Originally, Ashe had long, flowing white hair, but it proved too complicated to animate, so the team gave her a shorter, asymmetrical hairstyle. "It gave her an edgier look," said Hill. "But I always tell people who are cosplaying Ashe that short-hair Ashe and long-hair Ashe are both accurate."

**OPPOSITE & RIGHT** In-progress sketches and concepts to define Ashe's final look.

**TOP RIGHT** The initial storyboard sketch that galvanized the concept of the Deadlock Gang.

**FOLLOWING PAGES** In-progress concept of the Deadlock Gang, based on the initial storyboard.

Hill had a vision for the gang and its leader, which he brought to senior storyboard artist Mio Del Rosario for a concrete visual. "Jason came to me, and he said, 'Okay, this is what I want,'" said Del Rosario. "He described a big omnic and then Ashe, wearing a wide brim hat and holding a rifle. He was already playing with ideas about how much of an opposite Ashe could be to McCree."

"I just wanted it to be a woman," said Hill. "At the time, there were a lot of male figures in *Overwatch*, and it felt like this was a great opportunity to add a very strong female character. The minute I started thinking about it, I could see long white hair, black trench coat, big black brimmed hat. It was kind of a classic Western bad-guy look, but as a female.

"And Mio went and did an illustration—a storyboard—and nailed it. And Jungah Lee did a bunch of phenomenal concepts based off of Mio's sketch, which made us realize that the trench coat and the long hair made her look like a vampire hunter—more Gothic than what we were looking for, especially in a sci-fi Western. But the final look isn't all that different."

Del Rosario's initial sketch also included Ashe's omnic sidekick, B.O.B., and the rest of the Deadlock Gang, and proved to be just as foundational for their design. "Ashe, B.O.B., all the Deadlock Gang imagery—everything was based on that one thumbnail that Mio did, and we just went from there," said VanderJagt. "Every time, the first thing we tried, it was like, 'That's it. That's the design.' It was just one of those magical things that happens once or twice in your career where everybody is in perfect alignment from the get-go."

Unlike some Overwatch characters who wear costumes that liken them to superheroes, Ashe is designed to look more down to earth. This reinforces one of the central ideas that Hill wanted to convey about the character: that she is a real person. "A lot of our characters wear costumes, like Reinhardt has armor," said Hill. "I don't see Ashe in a costume. She puts on what she's wearing today. Tomorrow, she might have a trench coat, or she might not wear the vest. I don't think of her as a superhero so much as a living, breathing person going through life."

DEADLOCK

## ULTIMATE B.O.B.

▲ Believe it or not, Ashe's right-hand omnic B.O.B. started off as a tall, lanky character. "I went through a lot of iterations for B.O.B. before we landed on the big, burly guy," said Del Rosario. "I remember there was a poster around the map where they have this lone gunslinger. And I was like, 'Oh, maybe B.O.B. is going to be like that.' But then one of the problems that I encountered was, he started to blend with Ashe, like there was no contrast between them."

Del Rosario went back to the drawing board and returned with a brawny bouncer that would evolve into B.O.B. "I wanted him to be a machine, but with a little bit of gentleness to him," said Del Rosario. "So I put a mustache on him to make him like a gentleman. And a bowler hat. That was a last-minute thing."

Everyone instantly loved B.O.B., including the game designers tasked with concepting Ashe and her abilities. "B.O.B. was such a compelling character design," said *Overwatch*'s game director, Jeff Kaplan. "We had two designers take a stab at the in-game version of Ashe at the same time. And the whole team was excited to see how she was going to manifest in the game as a hero. There was some obvious stuff. Like her rifle was very distinct. But the coolest moment was when both of the designers unveiled their version of Ashe, they both had B.O.B. as her ultimate ability. It was really funny because you would have thought B.O.B. could have been his own hero." ▼

**LEFT** Concept of B.O.B.

**TOP & OPPOSITE** Concepts of the Deadlock Gang members.

EXPLORE T
ROUT
US

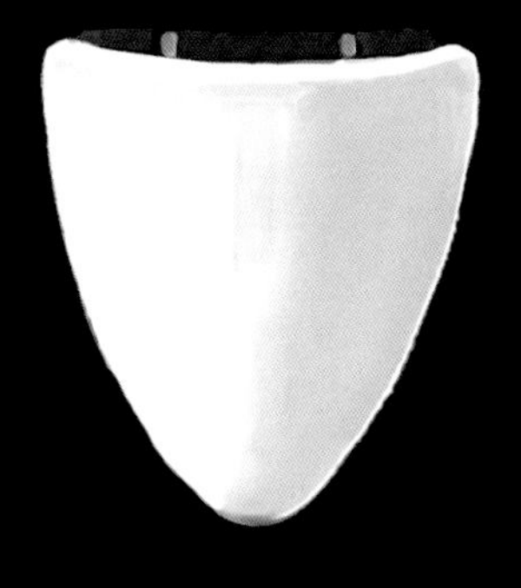

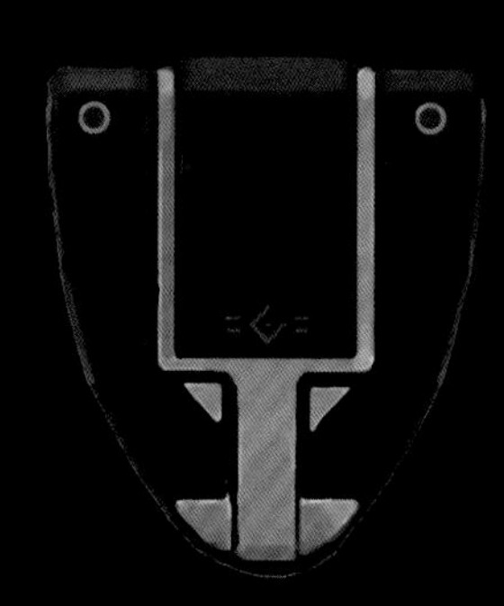

## DID YOU HEAR THAT?

The character Echo initially provided the entire premise for the cinematic—she's the payload riding on the train passing through town, which both McCree and the Deadlock Gang are after. But she quickly got relegated to second fiddle as the confrontation between McCree and Ashe took over as the dramatic core of the film. "The funny thing about 'Reunion' is that the story was supposed to launch Echo," said creative director & vice president of story and franchise development Jeff Chamberlain. "But the thing is, everybody loved Ashe so much she was released with it, and then Echo was postponed."

In fact, the filmmakers ended up designing the cinematic so that viewers would forget about the precious cargo on the train and be surprised by the reveal at the end. "Echo is the thing that the piece is actually designed for you to forget about," said Hill. "At the beginning, we have a shot that shows McCree reaching for a mug, and then there's a little chip on the table next to it. And he grabs it on the way out, and then we never reference it again. And the fight starts. So by the time you get back to him opening the crate containing Echo, the viewer has forgotten about it. It totally threw people. I didn't want the viewer to see that coming."

"This is one of the few pieces that you come out of with more questions than you went in with," said principal writer Andrew Robinson. "You've got Ashe, who is part of McCree's past, and the brief exchange that we have between Echo and McCree also indicates a past. Who is she? What happened? And she asks him a bunch of questions—questions that the audience has been asking like, 'What happened to his arm?' Those things will spur more game development, more character development."

LEFT Final render of the tabletop in the diner where McCree sets down the chip that will activate Echo.

ABOVE Concepts of the chip that McCree uses to activate Echo.

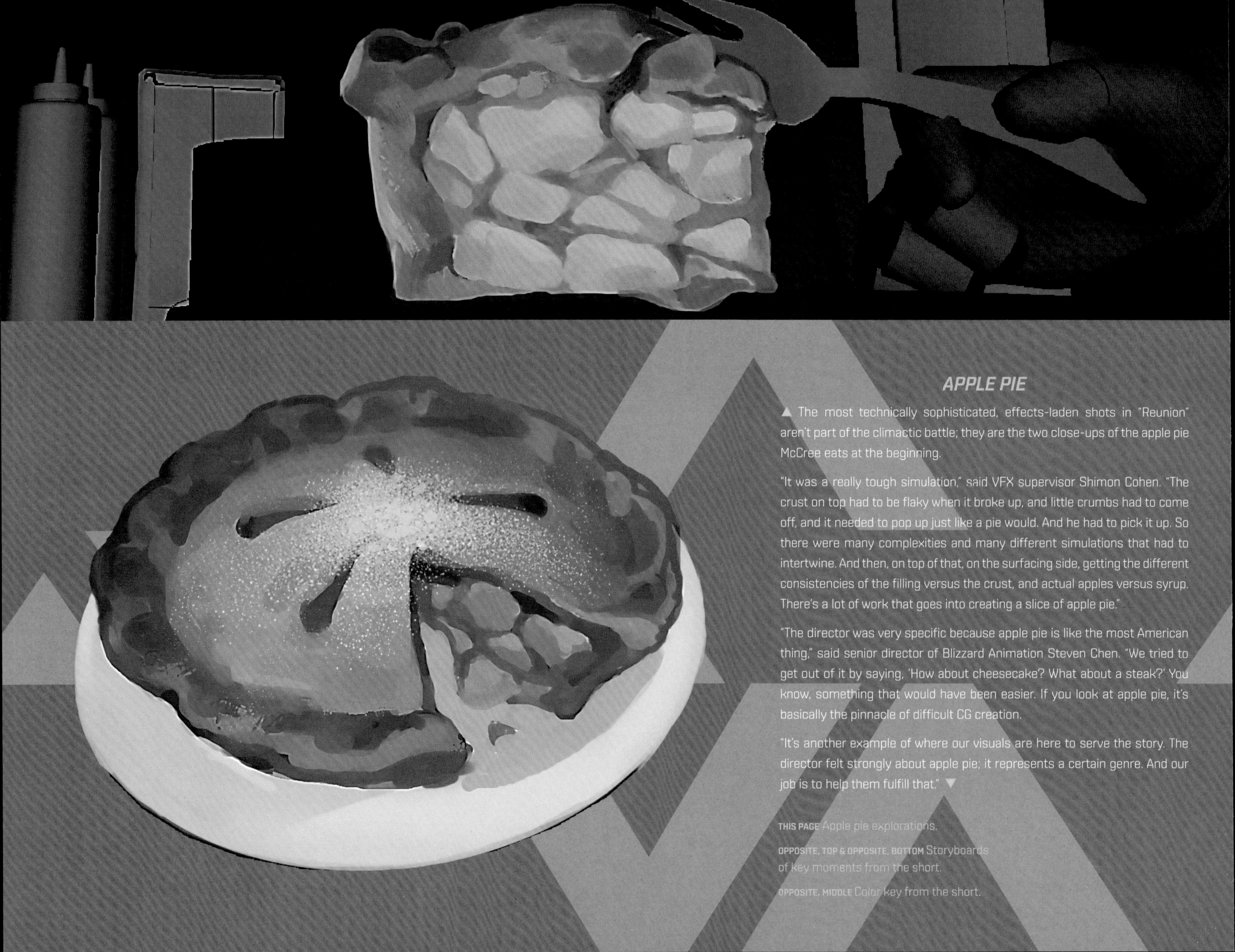

## APPLE PIE

▲ The most technically sophisticated, effects-laden shots in "Reunion" aren't part of the climactic battle; they are the two close-ups of the apple pie McCree eats at the beginning.

"It was a really tough simulation," said VFX supervisor Shimon Cohen. "The crust on top had to be flaky when it broke up, and little crumbs had to come off, and it needed to pop up just like a pie would. And he had to pick it up. So there were many complexities and many different simulations that had to intertwine. And then, on top of that, on the surfacing side, getting the different consistencies of the filling versus the crust, and actual apples versus syrup. There's a lot of work that goes into creating a slice of apple pie."

"The director was very specific because apple pie is like the most American thing," said senior director of Blizzard Animation Steven Chen. "We tried to get out of it by saying, 'How about cheesecake? What about a steak?' You know, something that would have been easier. If you look at apple pie, it's basically the pinnacle of difficult CG creation.

"It's another example of where our visuals are here to serve the story. The director felt strongly about apple pie; it represents a certain genre. And our job is to help them fulfill that." ▼

**THIS PAGE** Apple pie explorations.

**OPPOSITE, TOP & OPPOSITE, BOTTOM** Storyboards of key moments from the short.

**OPPOSITE, MIDDLE** Color key from the short.

## STANDOFF

▲ Following the lead of some of the most famous spaghetti Westerns, "Reunion" includes a tense standoff where time dilates and the characters watch one another for what feels like an eternity until they explode into action. Paradoxically, making a character stand still convincingly is one of the harder things to do in animation. "We call it 'keep alive' because they've got to still look like they're alive," said animation supervisor Hunter Grant.

The difficulty stems from the fact that if the characters don't move, they don't look alive. But if they are to move—even to glance around or take a breath—it has to be for a reason. "With a keep alive, they have to still look like they are thinking," said Grant. "So every time they blink, every time there's an eye twitch, every time there's an eye dart, any shift—it effectively reflects a thought."

Hill, though, wanted to dial back the typical keep alive in order to create an eerie stillness about the standoff—enough to make the viewer fidget. "During the standoff, where the characters were looking at each other, the animators kept adding extra little movements to keep alive, and I kept saying, 'Take that out; make them more still.' I know it went against every instinct they had, but we were trying to create a sense of uncomfortable tension." ▼

**TOP & OPPOSITE, TOP** Color keys from the short.

**MIDDLE** Final render of McCree firing.

**BOTTOM & OPPOSITE, BOTTOM** Storyboards of key moments in the standoff sequence.

## ENVISIONING ECHO

▲ Bringing Echo to the screen for the first time was challenging because she is made of materials that don't exist in real life: a hard white shell that looks like porcelain but absorbs light rather than reflects it, and blue "hard light," which appears to be a solid surface made of three-dimensional light, like a hologram.

Echo's white carapace was derived from the mysterious payload that the environment artists had created for the Route 66 map. "When we made the payload for Route 66, it was this military-looking device. And there was just this wooden crate on it," said *Overwatch*'s assistant art director Dion Rogers. "And *Overwatch*'s art director, Bill Petras, was like, 'Can we do something more interesting?' So one of the artists made this white technology egg. Later, we came up with the idea that it potentially could be Echo inside."

The team had made hard-light surfaces before, such as the displays in Watchpoint: Gibraltar and Ecopoint: Antarctica, but those had been two-dimensional surfaces. "The complexity came with having a 3D shape," said Cohen. "A flat plane is easy because there's no depth change. But Echo's face has lots of contours, lots of different shapes within it. You can see her eyes, you can see her mouth, you can see her teeth, yet she's transparent. To create that, we had to balance depth in a transparent object while still creating opaqueness in certain areas." ▼

"Reunion," which takes place at the characteristically Western high noon, offered a rather different color and lighting scenario than the other Overwatch prerendered cinematics, many of which happen at night. "We have a harsh desert sunlight for most of the show, trying to stay close to the vibe of the game map," said former art director Mathias Verhasselt. "And then we switch to a soft golden hour for the more calm and intimate last part, when McCree meets with Echo for the first time in a while."

**RIGHT** Color key of McCree leaving Echo.

# ORIGIN STORIES

THREE

**MOVING INTO THE YEAR FOLLOWING GAME RELEASE, THE OVERWATCH TEAM REEXAMINED THE ORIGIN-STORY FORMAT THEY HAD CREATED USING 2.5D MOTION-STORY ANIMATION.** The team wanted to continue to push the format creatively, as well as begin to streamline the production process.

The origin stories had started as almost spontaneous productions outside the typical cinematic pipeline, proceeding without formal storyboarding, previsualization, or effects work. While they were subject to executive guidance from game director Jeff Kaplan and art director Bill Petras, the development process was relatively loose.

Once the game launched, this informal methodology quickly became unsustainable. "I think the reality of having launched this game and having to keep up with the live content, the team just got really busy," said character art director Arnold Tsang. "And we were looking for ways for other artists to be able to devote their attention to making these as cool as we wanted them to be."

**LEFT** Final illustration of a Talon meeting from the Moira origin story.

The solution was to start to formalize the process by running the origin stories through the same steps as other cinematic productions, which made it possible to incorporate more and more creators, including storyboard artists, motion-story artists, editors, and directors. One cinematic—the Doomfist origin—even went full 2D anime with help from a Chinese studio called Wolfsmoke. This expansion of the origin stories pipeline allowed them to become as varied and exciting as the characters they depict.

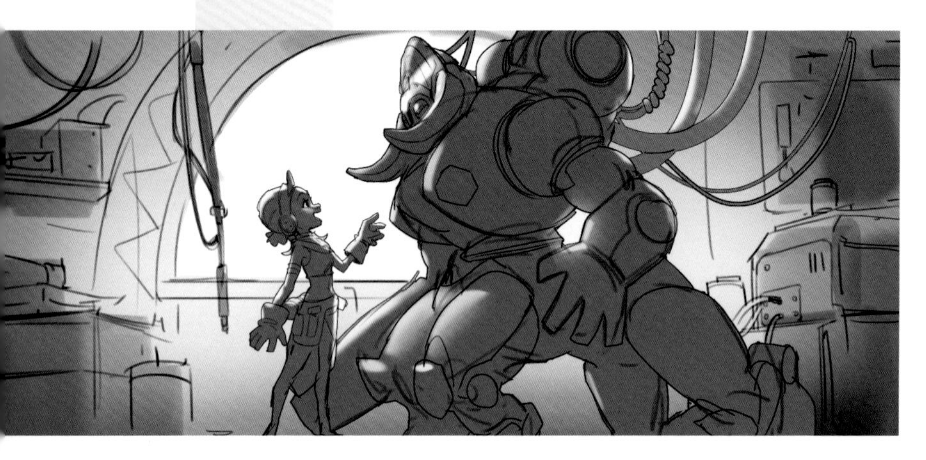

TOP LEFT Sketch for one of the illustrations from the Orisa origin story.

BOTTOM LEFT Storyboard from the Doomfist origin story.

TOP RIGHT Early sketch for one of the illustrations from the Sigma origin story.

## BEADS ON A STRING

One of the things that makes the origin stories stimulating for the creators is the flexibility of the format. The 2.5D motion story is quick and accommodates iteration in ways that the 3D pipeline doesn't. It's relatively easy, for example, to adjust a script during editing, rerecord audio, and find a better fit between voiceover and imagery.

This means that an origin story can begin with a rough outline and then be refined through cycles of review and incremental adjustments that allow the hero in question to emerge. "The creation of these pieces starts really early in the character development process. We're figuring out aspects of these characters, like their personality and their backstory, and start working on these with loose ideas," said *Overwatch*'s former lead writer Michael Chu, who wrote the majority of the origin stories. "As the iteration process goes on, the voice of the character and what's important to them—like their internal conflict or their internal interest—starts to take over."

The freedom of the format also allows the creators to reference a new character or location without having to go through a complete 3D development process, either in game or in cinematic. This supports rapid world building, much like with books, comics, and other types of relatively "fast" media, but using a moving-image format that feels live and authentic to a character's point of view.

"These characters have lots of different connections and relationships to other people and the universe, and a lot of them are pretty defining," said Chu. "So I think not only having the character talk about themselves but also about how they relate to the other characters in the cast helps to add depth. We see them not just as opportunities to tell the story of the characters but also to make the universe bigger."

## WHAT IS AN ORIGIN STORY?

As the team explored the format, they began to engage in storytelling that wasn't so much about a character's origins per se—i.e., delivering information about how they became a hero—but rather their point of view.

"You can kind of see with different heroes that sometimes the films are more about the personality, sometimes they're more about the backstory, sometimes they're about both," said Chu. "For each one, it was sort of identifying what it was that we wanted to get across. One of the challenges was always trying to figure out how to do that in four or five images."

"You have to tell a story in a medium that is very succinct," said director Jeramiah Johnson, who helmed the Baptiste and Sigma pieces. "It's funny, simple is actually really hard. Because it's a 2.5D motion story, people think, 'Oh, it's just a small thing.' But if you really boil it down, the heart is what you're trying to communicate—what you want the audience to experience in the most entertaining way possible."

While the approach to each origin story may be different, the overall goal of the origin stories remains consistent. "We now release the origin stories with the launch of a new character, so it's a fan's first experience of a character," said Johnson. "So while I don't feel like we have to check every box, we have to check the big boxes so you walk away, and you're like, 'Okay, I know who that character is.' It's really about getting the fans excited and letting them know who a hero is—who you might be stepping into when you play them or face off against them."

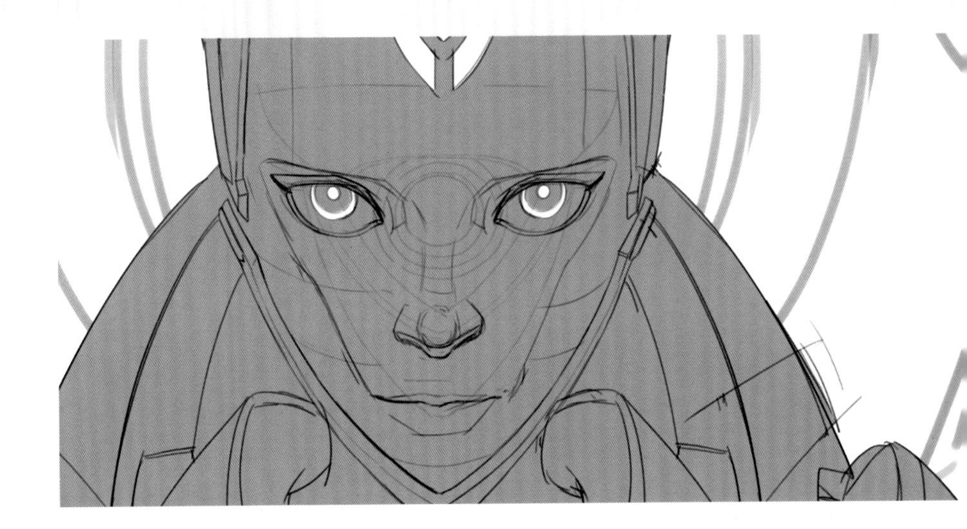

**TOP LEFT** Early sketches exploring moments from the Brigitte origin story.

**MIDDLE LEFT** In-progress illustration of the final frame in the Wrecking Ball origin story.

**BOTTOM LEFT** In-progress illustration from the Ashe origin piece.

**BOTTOM RIGHT** Sketch of the final frame in the Echo origin story.

# ORISA

"WE WERE ABLE TO COME UP WITH AN ELEGANT POWER-ON SEQUENCE. YOU HEAR HER DESCRIBED IN ANOTHER CHARACTER'S WORDS, BUT AT THE END, ORISA SPEAKS FOR HERSELF."

—MICHAEL CHU, FORMER LEAD WRITER

**UP UNTIL ORISA'S ORIGIN STORY, WHICH WAS RELEASED ON** March 2, 2017, the 2.5D character-driven motion stories had been narrated exclusively by the heroes they introduce. For Orisa, a robot, the team decided instead to start her tale with the voice of her creator, a young robotics prodigy named Efi Oladele from Numbani. "I was always a proponent of us not falling into patterns with these—like we should vary the use of color or the narrator," said *Overwatch*'s former lead writer, Michael Chu. "That kept them feeling fresh."

Besides offering a variation that hadn't been tried before, beginning with Efi's point of view also made sense in the context of the piece. Having Orisa as the original narrator immediately raised the question: How would she be able to tell what led up to her activation if she wasn't conscious prior to that moment? "It was like, 'Well, where do we start with this?' Because in order for Orisa to be doing all the dialogue, she'd have to be self-aware of how she came to be," said former editor Nathan Schauf, who edited and codirected the piece.

Efi not only resolved this logical conundrum; she also allowed the Overwatch team to expand the scope of the piece. By incorporating her viewpoint, the filmmakers were able to seed in more history about the threats facing Numbani, such as the failure of the squad of OR15 defense robots to protect the city from a recent attack by Doomfist.

**RIGHT** Sketch of Efi working on Orisa.

HOLOGRAPH
SCREEN

An early version of the script depicted Doomfist's attack in the present tense, with Orisa defending the city against him. "There actually was going to be a shot of Orisa fighting Doomfist," said Chu. "We ended up taking it out because throwing in a character like Doomfist really sucks up all the attention. Like if you saw a picture where they are fighting, it wouldn't really be about Orisa anymore. Also, Orisa is built to fight Doomfist, so if you've already seen them going head to head, it's like you skipped to the final boss battle."

On a character level, Efi completes Orisa, a robot whose primary function is to protect the people of Numbani. "Orisa conceptually was a challenging character for the team," said Chu. "We never really felt like we had cracked the code on her until we added Efi. Seeing Orisa as the creation of this other character really helped encapsulate her. It helped us figure out her behaviors and attitudes."

Prior to the introduction of Efi, Orisa was a bit one dimensional, although her fundamental innocence was carried through to the final piece. "The way Orisa was pitched to us was like a Great Dane that still thinks it's a puppy," said Schauf. "That was the inspiration for the bus shot. She's protecting this old lady but ruining a bunch of other stuff in the process."

**TOP RIGHT** Sketch of Efi talking to Orisa.

**BOTTOM RIGHT** In-progress illustration of Efi working on Orisa.

**TOP & BOTTOM** Storyboards depicting possible moments in Orisa's origin story, some of which were left out, such as Efi finding a part in a junkyard [top middle] and a confrontation between Orisa and Doomfist [bottom right].

**MIDDLE** In-progress illustration of Efi talking to Orisa.

**FOLLOWING PAGES** Final illustration of the second-to-last shot in Orisa's origin piece.

## THE HERO'S FORMAT

▲ Although the Overwatch team tried to push the envelope each time they made a new origin story, certain conventions that have remained in place were established with the Orisa piece.

For one, it is the first origin that starts with a character icon at the beginning—an element that has become a defining feature of the character-driven motion stories. Second, Orisa's origin ends on a hero pose that mirrors the stance she takes during character selection in the game.

Establishing this framework really helped instigate production and quicken the pace for the creation of other origin stories. "We can start drawing that closing shot right now. Its length will be based on the dialogue, but we already know what we're going to do," said Schauf. "Once we decided that, we were like, 'Okay, this is how we're going to do these from now on. They'll start the same and they'll end the same. But anything in the middle will be completely up for grabs.'" ▼

**ABOVE** Orisa's badge, similar to a version that appears at the beginning of her origin story.

**LEFT** Final illustration of Orisa striking a heroic pose.

# DOOMFIST

"THIS IS THE STORY DOOMFIST TELLS ABOUT WHAT HE DID THAT DAY. IT'S EXAGGERATED. YOU SHOULDN'T LET THE TRUTH GET IN THE WAY OF A GOOD STORY."

—DOUG GREGORY, DIRECTOR

**FOR DOOMFIST'S ORIGIN STORY, RELEASED ON JULY 6,** 2017, the team wanted to do something momentous—to create a piece that would capture the imposing stature of the Talon member and establish him as a force to be reckoned with in the Overwatch universe. This mandate demanded something different, which made Doomfist's origin a perfect fit for 2D anime and its larger-than-life approach to storytelling. "I look at this as a tall-tale version of events," said director Doug Gregory. "That's what anime does well. They're stories exaggerated by the tellers."

In the case of Doomfist's origin, the teller is Doomfist himself. "To me, the tall-tale approach seemed to fit Doomfist pretty well," said Gregory. "He's not going to say, 'I just punched some guy.' He's going say, 'I knocked him ten blocks down the street.'"

The story premise was basic—a jailbreak and a fight that pitted Doomfist against some of the most recognizable Overwatch characters to date: Winston, Tracer, and Genji. But it's told from Doomfist's myth-making point of view. "He punches himself out of jail," said Gregory. "So you kind of automatically ask the question, 'Why didn't he do that before?' It's like on that day, he decided, 'Yeah,

RIGHT Layout drawing of Doomfist in the street.

_C16
BG
B
A

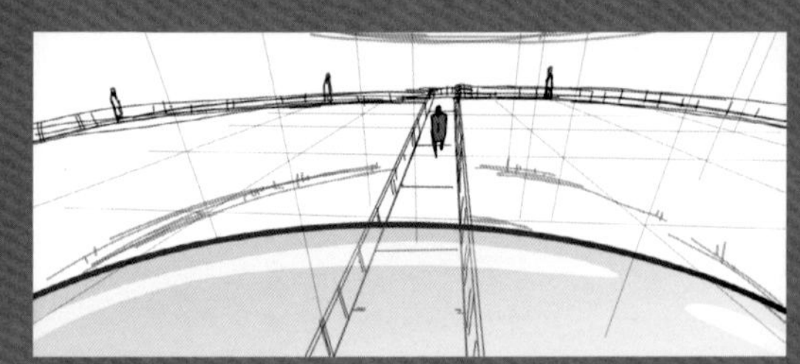

I'm ready to go. I've had my break.' And the other big thing we wanted to get across is that when we say Doomfist, it's not just the glove that he wears. He can still punch through walls. The glove exaggerates what he already is inside."

To make this larger-than-life anime, Blizzard wanted to connect with a talented studio that specializes in the medium. Cloud and Clover, the two heads of China's Wolfsmoke Studio, sprang to mind. After touring the Blizzard campus in 2016, they had started periodically sending Gregory fan art depicting Overwatch characters, demonstrating that they had a deep understanding of who the characters were, as well as Overwatch's overarching visual style.

To start production, some definition of what it meant to do anime Overwatch style had to be established. "Anime is inherently rebellious. It's a medium that's meant to be free-spirited," said Gregory. "If you had a character in Overwatch do some of the crazy stuff you see in some anime battles, we would go, 'Well, that's too far.' We couldn't actually use the full breadth of that particular canon. So we had to find the right partner who was willing to work within brackets.

"We wound up doing the first pass of storyboards on our side of the ocean, so to speak. We storyboarded it very broadly—the basic beats of the story. And then the thing that Wolfsmoke really added was the sense of timing, taking it to the next level by making that punch snap a little bit more in your face or giving a little bit of airtime to when Doomfist jumps up before he smashes down.

"There's a lot of great movement thanks to what Cloud and Clover brought to the table with their team. It's exactly the way I wanted Doomfist introduced: it's the mythic version of him."

**THIS PAGE** Storyboards of a confrontation between Doomfist and a prison guard, which was left out of the final origin story.

**OPPOSITE, TOP** Layout drawings of Doomfist's escape from prison.

**OPPOSITE, BOTTOM** Layout drawings of Doomfist's confrontation with Winston and Tracer.

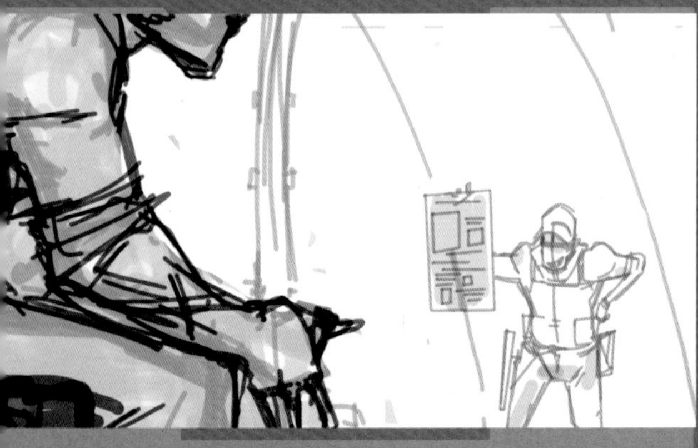

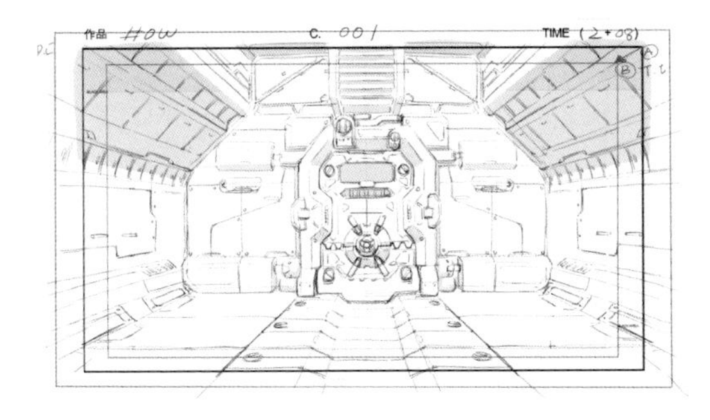

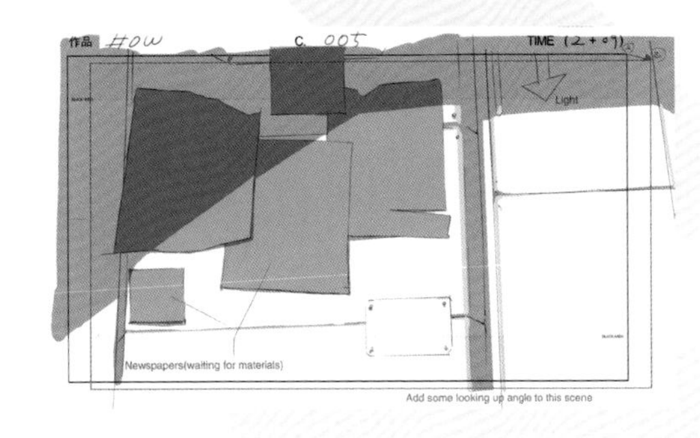



## WOLFSMOKE

▲ Gregory had met Cloud and Clover of Wolfsmoke at an industry conference in 2016. Co-owners of the studio, Cloud works as lead animator and director while Clover acts as producer and art director. They had become well known in animation circles thanks to their short "Kung Fu Cooking Girls" (2011) and were exhibiting at the show.

"I met them, and they were really, really cool," said Gregory. "They mentioned something about wanting to come take a tour of Blizzard. I offered to introduce them to the Overwatch team because they're big fans. So I took them over, and I introduced them. And then about a month later, I got a call from Jeff Chamberlain, saying he wanted to talk to them about doing an anime. I just showed up at the right time with the right people. It was chocolate and peanut butter." ▼

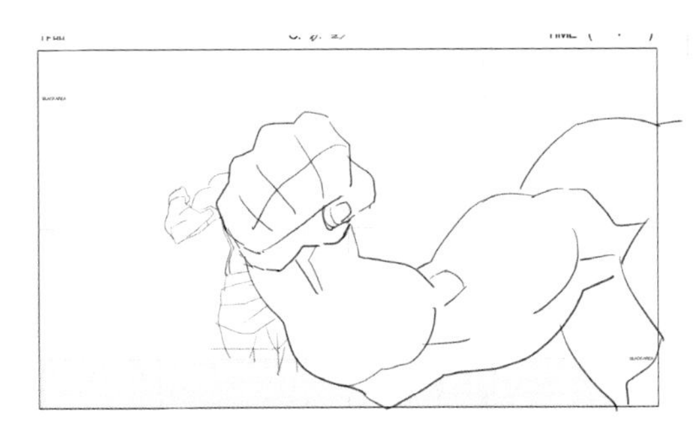

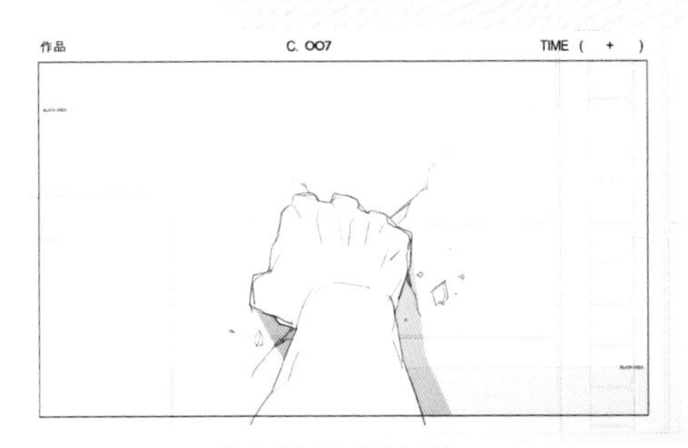



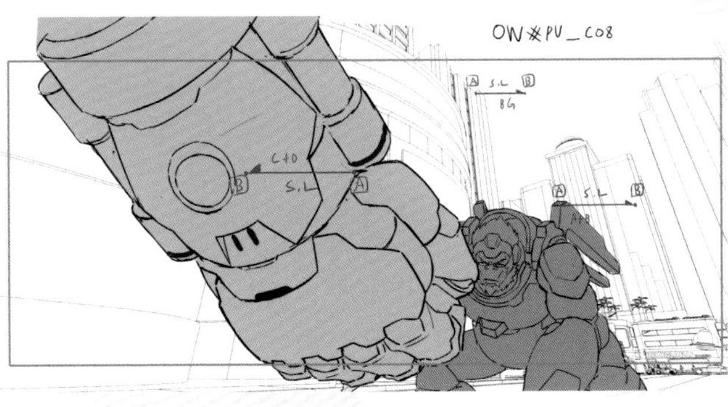

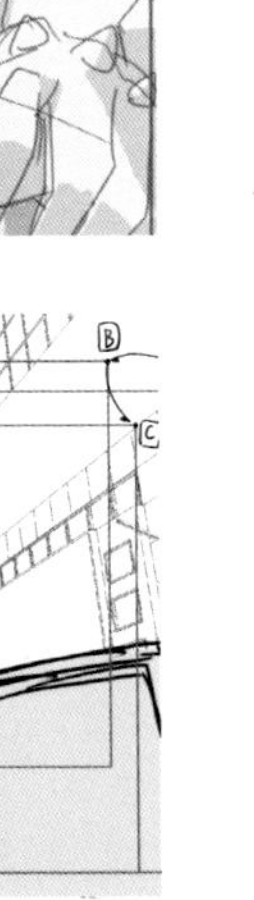

**OPPOSITE, TOP** Layout drawing of Doomfist.

**THIS PAGE** Explorations of action sequences in the film.

**LEFT** Final image of Doomfist preparing to punch Winston.

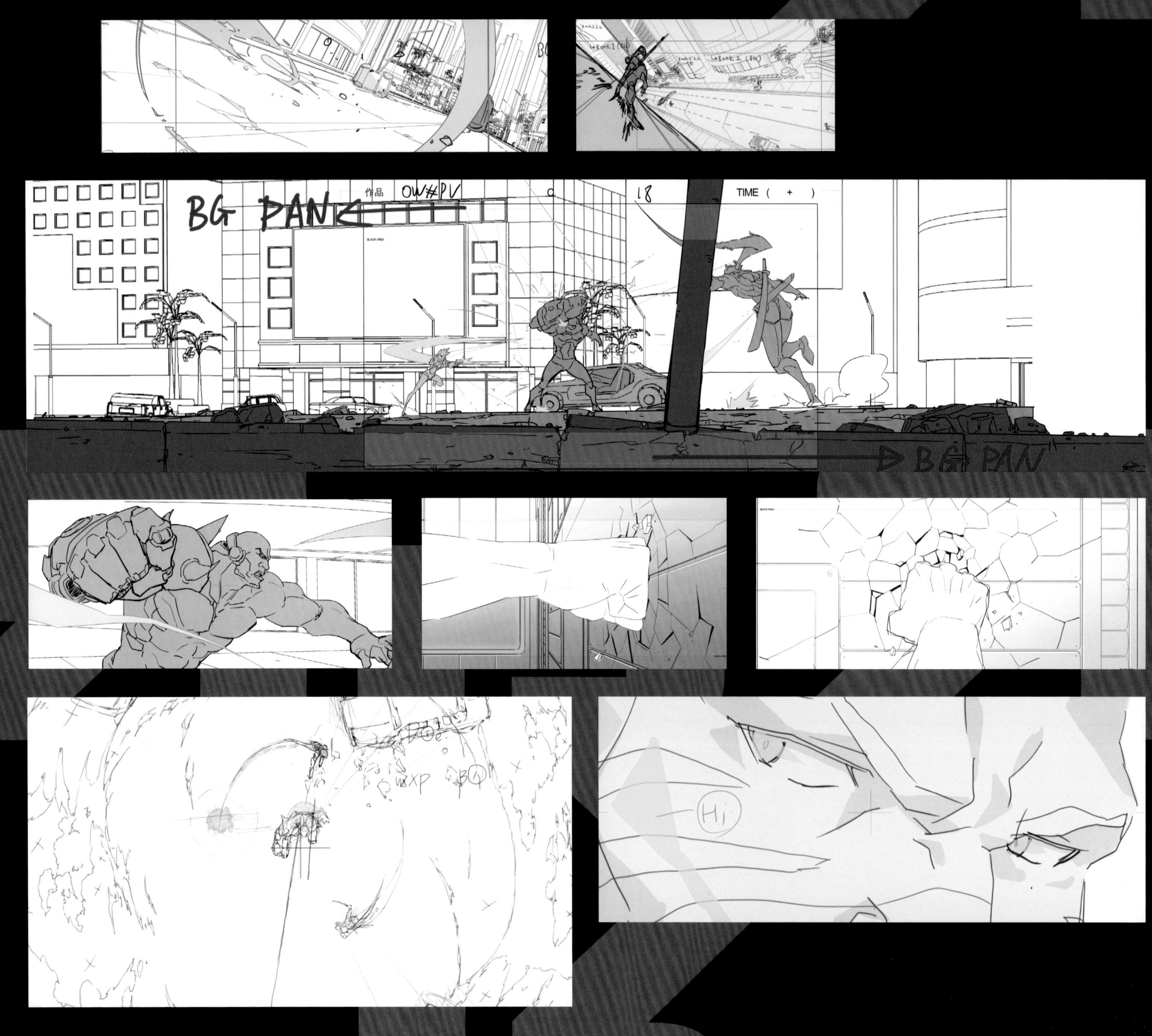
BG PAN
作品 OW#PV
TIME ( + )
BG PAN
Hi

**THESE PAGES** Storyboards and layout drawings depicting key moments in the cinematic.

**THESE PAGES** Layout drawings used to choreograph the action in the film.

**BELOW** Image of Doomfist pausing to get a read on Tracer's location.

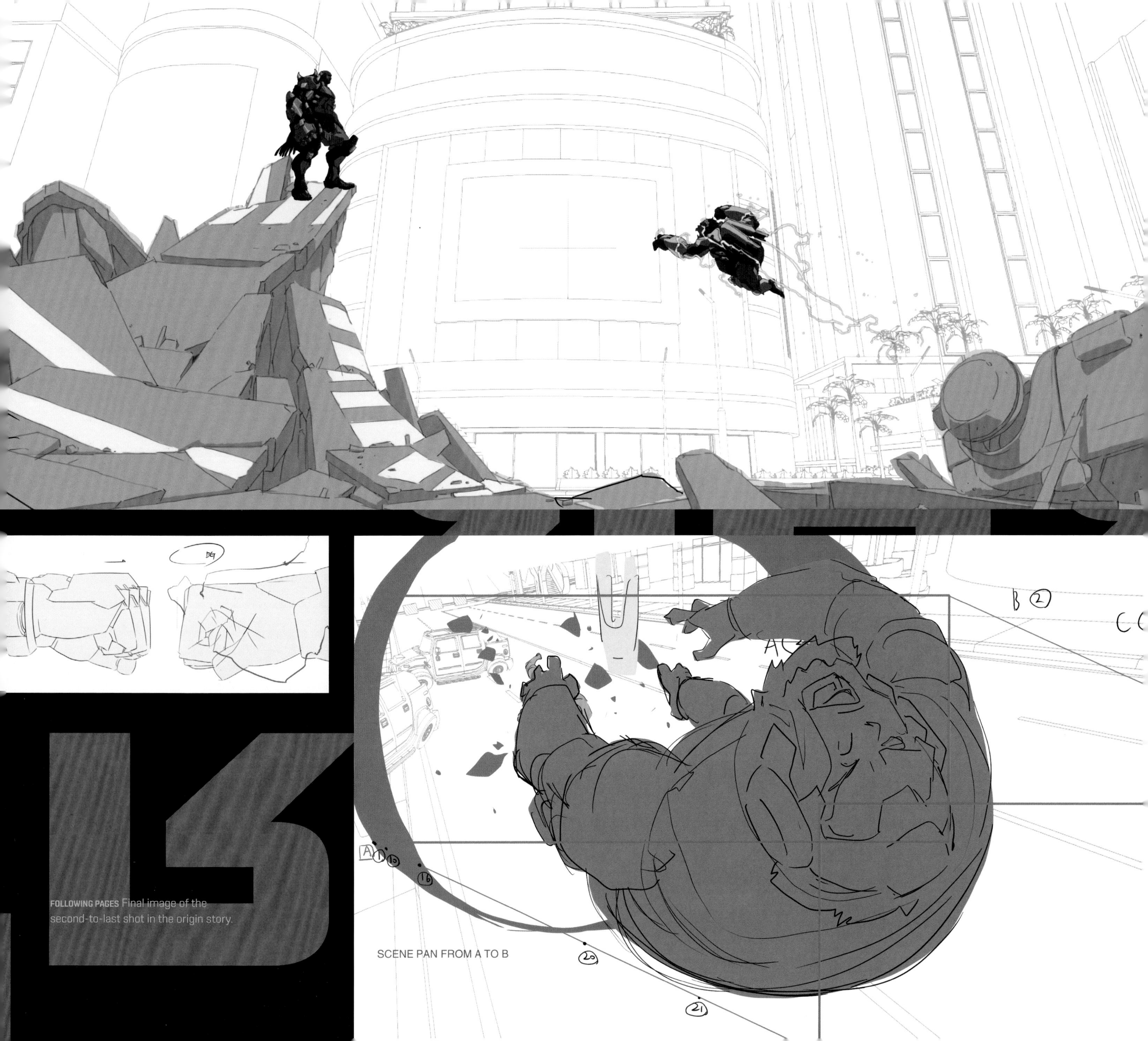


**FOLLOWING PAGES** Final image of the second-to-last shot in the origin story.

# MOIRA

"MOST OF THE TIME, I FOCUS ON THE CHARACTERS. I ILLUSTRATE VERY STYLIZED CHARACTERS AGAINST REALISTIC BACKGROUNDS."

—NESSKAIN, VISUAL DEVELOPMENT ARTIST

**IN MOIRA'S ORIGIN STORY, RELEASED ON NOVEMBER 3, 2017,** the Overwatch team began to experiment with the play between image and voiceover. Unlike the other characters who preceded her, Moira is a bit of an unreliable narrator—a person whose perspective on reality doesn't quite line up with what most others perceive. "If you look at the earlier ones, the imagery and the words always worked together," said *Overwatch*'s former lead writer, Michael Chu. "And then we realized the image doesn't always have to directly pertain to the words. In the Moira one, she has an idea of how things are going, and the world has sort of a different idea of how things are going. And I think that juxtaposition is what makes that one really interesting."

For example, a noticeable disconnect between words and image is the shot where Moira is working on Gabriel Reyes. Her voiceover confidently comments, "Together, we delved deeper into those areas forbidden by law, by morality, and by fear." Meanwhile, Reyes, who is starting to turn into insubstantial shadow, presaging his transformation into Reaper, looks rather disturbed and unsure of what is happening to him.

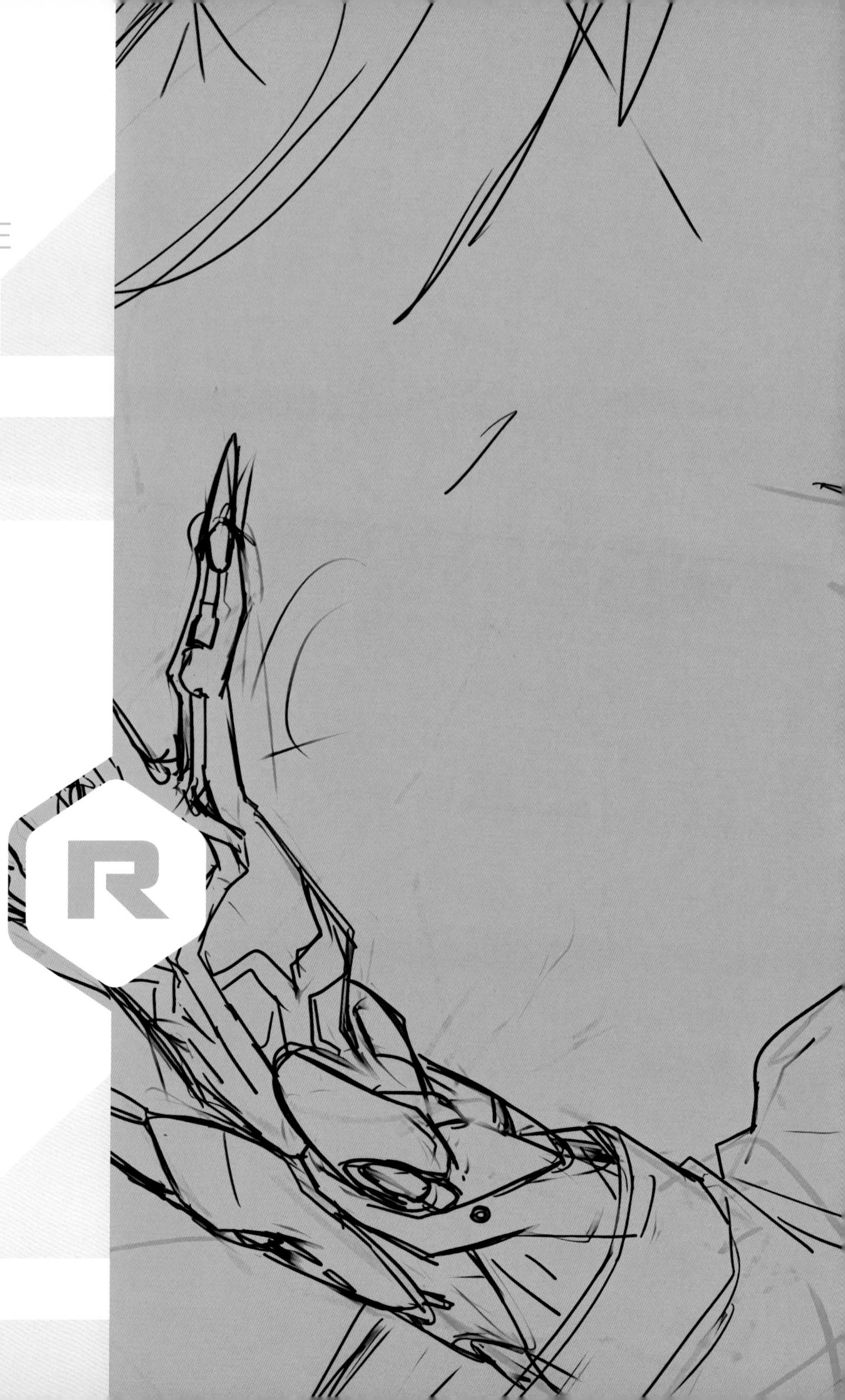

**RIGHT** Sketch for the final illustration in Moira's origin story.

THIS PAGE, OPPOSITE, TOP & OPPOSITE, BOTTOM Sketches for several illustrations in the origin story.

OPPOSITE, MIDDLE Illustration of Moira conducting experiments on Reyes.

Moira's origin story is, in a way, Reaper's origin as well, suggesting that Moira is the one who imbued Reyes with one of his most iconic powers, Wraith Form. The cinematic also features cameos from Genji, McCree, Doomfist, and the Talon agent Maximilien, subtly delivering a significant amount of backstory that intimates Moira has been involved with three of the major organizations in the Overwatch universe—Overwatch, Blackwatch, and Talon—although her exact relationships remain unclear.

A lot of this information is conveyed during the panoramic opening sequence, which includes four interrelated shots that take place against the backdrop of one long, continuous background painting of Moira's lab. This complex progression was particularly challenging to figure out. "Originally, we were looking down the hallway with Moira in front," said former editor Nathan Schauf, who edited and codirected the piece. "Knowing the 2.5D medium, I was like, 'That's going to be really hard to pull off without really fast transitions.' So I said, 'Let's try to do time lapse in this one massive shot.' We changed the orientation, started to pan, and made it so she would fade out and then fade in."

Approaching the first shot this way slowed down the pacing so the visuals could match the timing of the voiceover. The illustrator, Nesskain, who had become a major artist for the Overwatch origin stories by that point, had to create a single, complex painting that accounted for all the different camera and character movements. "It was the first time they asked me to do a panorama shot where you're panning the camera from left to right," said Nesskain. "On top of that, there were four different changes for the character and the lighting. It was a lot to deal with in one illustration."

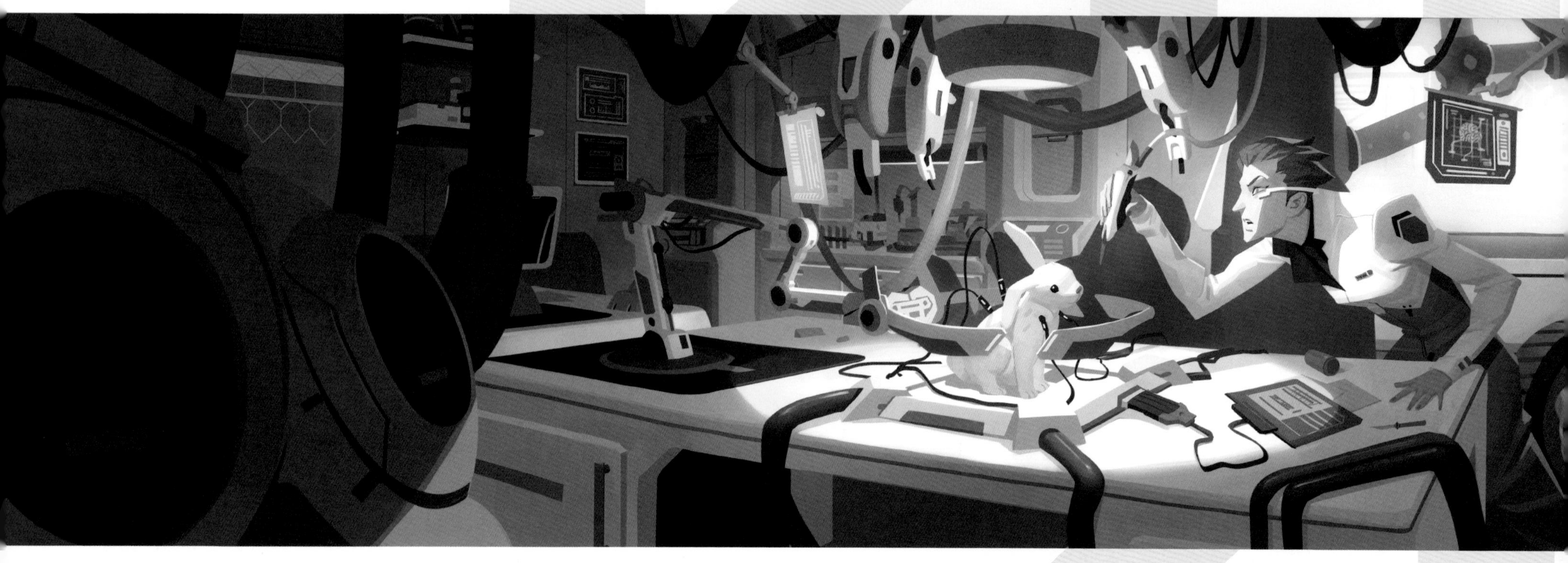

**THESE PAGES** Final and in-progress illustrations used to create the origin story's opening panning shot.

**FOLLOWING PAGES** Illustration of Moira meeting Reyes, Genji, and McCree outside of a Blackwatch dropship.

EXIT
E-8

EXIT

EXIT

BW-14

### NESSKAIN

▲ Kim-Seang Hong, who goes by Nesskain professionally, had been working for a long time on Overwatch conceptual artwork as a freelancer under the supervision of character art director Arnold Tsang. Well known in the comics world, Nesskain had caught Tsang's attention via his Overwatch fan art, which started a relationship that led to official contributions to the Blizzard property.

On Moira's origin story, Nesskain was given the opportunity to do all of the illustrations. Eventually, Nesskain was hired as a full-time artist by Blizzard, where he's worked consistently on Overwatch cinematics and illustrations. His art style has come to define the origin stories, particular his use of color. "I have a mathematical way of working since I'm color blind," said Nesskain. "The way I work with color is very binary. I choose one color to define the mood of the piece. Then, from that color, I add an opposing one on the color wheel, and so on. It's a reaction from one color to the next."

Nesskain's color blindness is only partial but causes him to avoid certain hues, as well as rely on the color pickers in the digital illustration programs he uses. "Certain greens can be yellow to me sometimes, and all the grays can be green to me as well," he said. "I try to avoid them most of the time. Fortunately, this is digital, so I can rely on the color selection tools. But if it was traditional, I wouldn't know how to mix colors." ▼

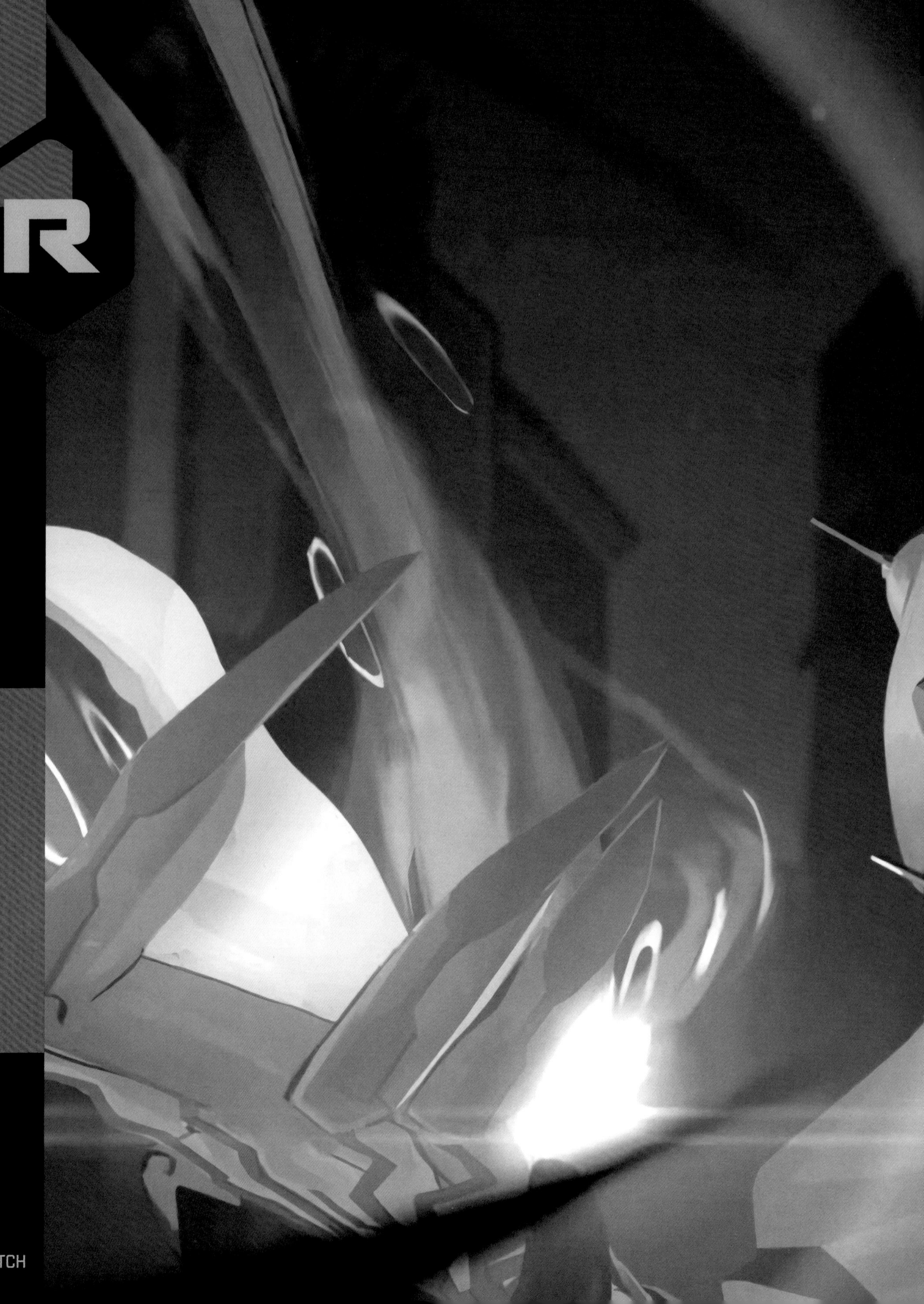

**RIGHT** Final illustration of Moira in the hero pose at the end of her origin story.

# BRIGITTE

"I THINK PEOPLE FINALLY REALIZED BRIGITTE IS TORBJÖRN'S DAUGHTER WITH THIS MOVIE. IT'S A VERY LONG ARC FROM HER INTRODUCTION TO SHOWING UP IN THE GAME."

—MICHAEL CHU, FORMER LEAD WRITER

**AFTER *OVERWATCH'S* LAUNCH IN 2016, ORIGIN STORY** cinematics started to be used to introduce new playable heroes. While this was true in the case of Brigitte, she was already a character familiar to the Overwatch audience, having appeared as Reinhardt's squire in the comic "Dragon Slayer" and the prerendered cinematic "Honor and Glory." With this established record, the team didn't need to introduce Brigitte so much as bring her from the background to the foreground, telling a tale that shows how she came into her own and emerged from the shadows of two existing heroes, her mentor Reinhardt and her father Torbjörn.

Because Nesskain, who had become the go-to artist for these productions following the Moira short, was busy at the time, character art director Arnold Tsang and fellow artist Ben Zhang, who had originally created the concept for Brigitte, jumped in to provide the art for the cinematic, which was released on February 28, 2018. "We were able to dip our toes back into doing the origin short for Brigitte, and it was really fun because by then, the process was so fluid," said Tsang. "Having other talented people devote time to writing the stories and come up with storyboards really matured the process. They really helped breathe life into it."

RIGHT Sketch for the opening illustration of Brigitte's origin story, which substantiates the longstanding connection between her, Reinhardt (left), and her father Torbjörn (right).

**TOP** Sketches for illustrations in the origin story.

**MIDDLE** In-progress illustrations for the origin piece.

**LEFT** Detail of pictures hanging in the Lindholm home in the opening shot of the film.

**OPPOSITE, TOP** Early sketch for the illustration showing Brigitte building Jetpack Cat.

**OPPOSITE, BOTTOM** Illustration of Brigitte working on Jetpack Cat in Torbjörn's workshop. Torbjörn works on Reinhardt's Rocket Hammer in the background.

This elevated creative approach shines through in how Brigitte's progression is communicated visually as well as narratively in the piece. "In the opening shot, we had Reinhardt in there where he's enormous and she's this little girl. And by the end of it, she's the one keeping Reinhardt together," said former editor Nathan Schauf, who edited and codirected the piece.

The last shot has Brigitte in the foreground, seen from below. She looks like a larger-than-life character contrasted with the smaller Reinhardt, whose gray armor fades into the smoke-filled background. "We wanted to make sure her color and her suit really popped," said Schauf. "She's on a battlefield in a pose that's super reminiscent of early Overwatch team illustrations."

## JETPACK CAT

▲ Jetpack Cat was an early hero concept that was scratched from Overwatch since it seemed too over the top, although the developers kept a special place for the flying feline in their hearts. When it came time to tell Brigitte's story, they felt like there was room for Jetpack Cat in official Overwatch lore, even if it wasn't as a hero.

"I think it started with someone jokingly saying, 'We should get Jetpack Cat in there,'" said Schauf. "It makes sense because the master engineer Torbjörn is Brigitte's dad, so of course, she has those skills too and can build her cat a jetpack. The drawing is great because it tells so much about her. And at the same time, you also see Torbjörn in the back working on Reinhardt's hammer. There's so much in that shot when you digest it." ▼

**ABOVE & RIGHT** Background props that appear in the illustration of Brigitte working on Jetpack Cat.

**FAR RIGHT & BOTTOM** Progression from early sketch (far right) to color illustration (bottom) in the origin story.

**OPPOSITE** Progression from early sketches (top left and top right) to color illustration (bottom).

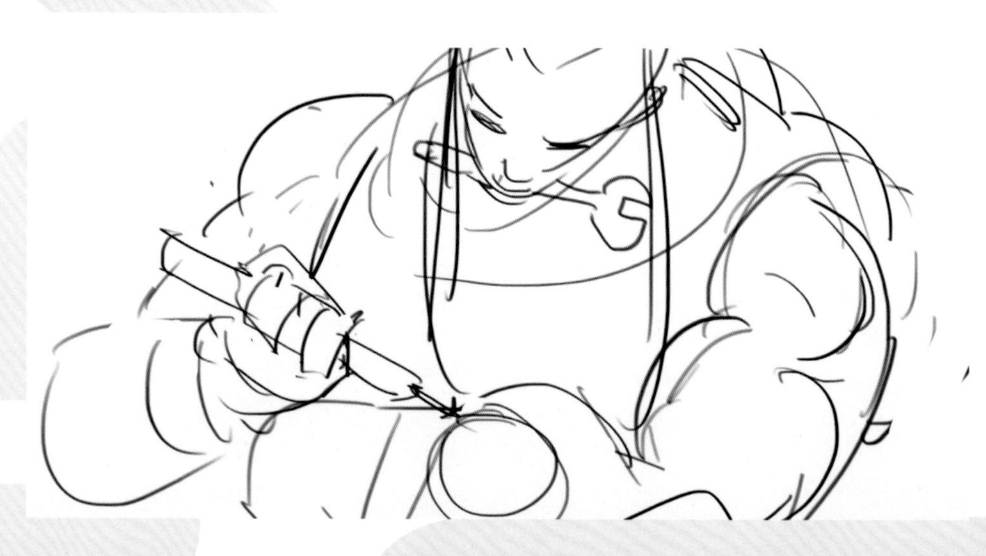

## TURNING CHARACTERS INTO HEROES

▲ Brigitte is probably the most prominent example of a tendency that has come to define Overwatch: a character is first introduced in a cameo and then emerges as a playable hero. "In general, there's this sense that because it's a hero game, cameo characters can become heroes in their own right. So we always try and imagine the role they could fill if they do someday," said *Overwatch*'s former lead writer Michael Chu. "When we debut a character that we feel like is going to be important to the story moving forward, we do an abbreviated version of the character creation process, where we try and figure out some aspects of their backstory, the kind of stuff that compels them, their wants and desires, and stuff like that—especially for a character like Brigitte because her story meshes with Reinhardt's."

"When we started coming up with hero prototypes for the next hero, eventually we landed on a paladin-type character," said Tsang. "And we wanted to blend the fantasy tropes from other Blizzard games with Overwatch. And then from there, it organically became the idea of making Brigitte that paladin character." ▼

**THIS PAGE** Sketch (above) and color illustration (right) for the last shot in the origin piece.

# WRECKING BALL

"THERE ARE MANY TIMES WHEN, FROM A CINEMATIC STORYTELLING PERSPECTIVE, WE MIGHT WANT TO TRY SOMETHING NEW."

—NATHAN SCHAUF, FORMER EDITOR

**AS A SENTIENT HAMSTER IN A MECH, WRECKING BALL IS A** character that pushes the limits of Overwatch. "He's a fun character, but a lot of people were like, 'Does he belong in the game? Is there a spot for him in the game?'" said former editor Nathan Schauf, who directed the character's origin story. "And *Overwatch*'s former creative director, Chris Metzen, came in and was just like, 'Yeah, he does. He's awesome.'"

With Wrecking Ball's presence firmly established, it became a question of creating a believable story that would explain how he came to be. "When we were talking about him, it was like, 'Well, how do you make a character like that feel like he belongs in the universe?'" said Michael Chu, who was *Overwatch*'s lead writer at the time. "So we had him pass through the gates of some of the more out-there parts of the Overwatch universe, starting in Horizon Lunar Colony, which we'd established as a place where there are genetically engineered animals, and then putting him through the crucible of Junkertown, where everything is sort of heightened and a little zany. With those touchpoints, a character like Wrecking Ball starts to make sense."

**RIGHT** Early sketch for the opening panoramic shot of the Wrecking Ball origin story.

LAUNCH BAY 14

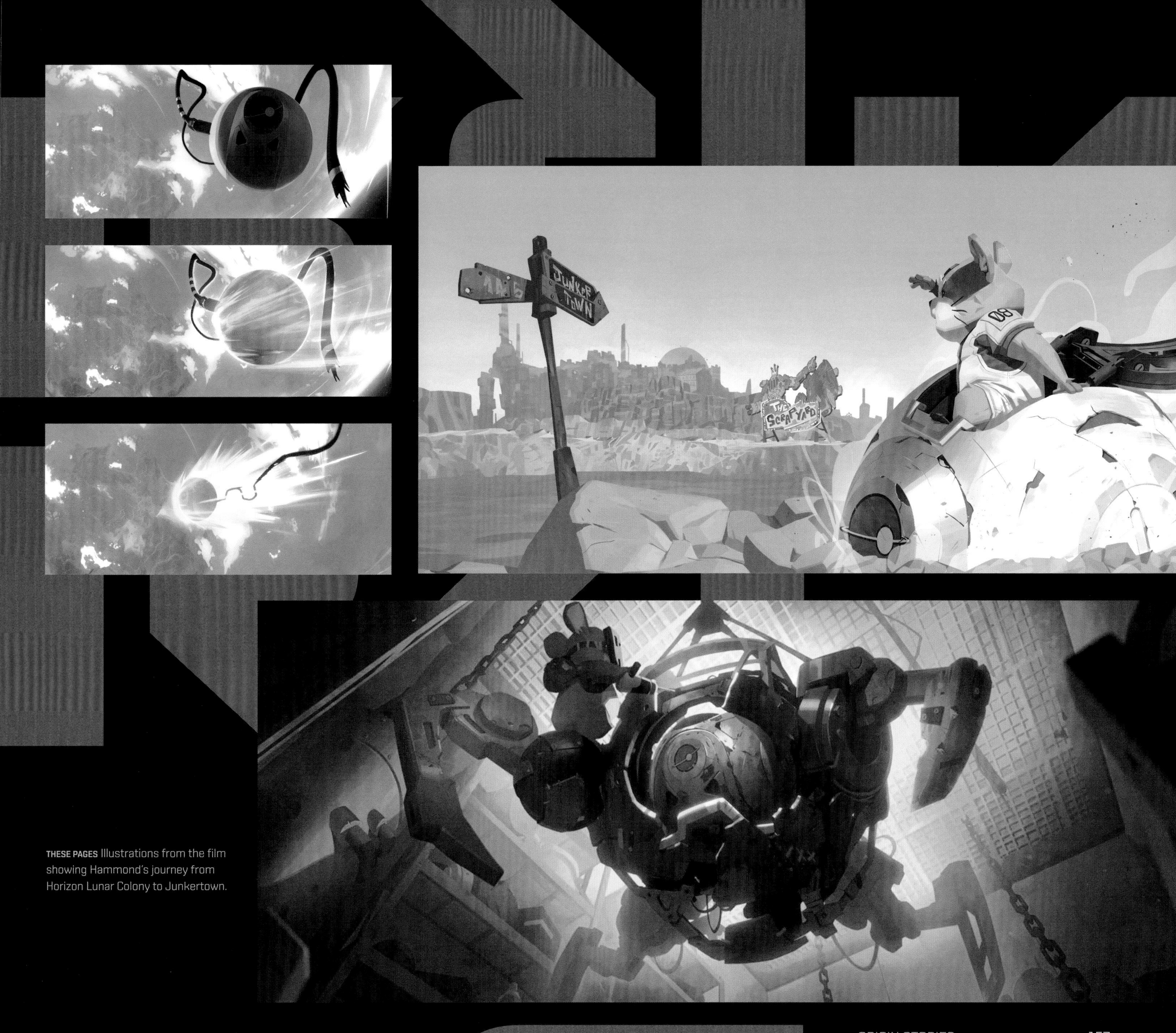


**THESE PAGES** Illustrations from the film showing Hammond's journey from Horizon Lunar Colony to Junkertown.

Working within this framework, the filmmakers set about filling in specifics. One of the first challenges they encountered was deciding who would narrate the piece since Wrecking Ball doesn't really talk or have a companion who could speak for him.

The idea emerged that Dr. Harold Winston—the scientist on Horizon Lunar Colony who had been introduced in "Recall"—would provide the voiceover by reading a journal entry about his early observations of Hammond, the hamster who would eventually become Wrecking Ball. The filmmakers wanted to play with a disconnect between what the doctor says about Hammond in the audio and what actually happens to Wrecking Ball during the course of the film, which was released on June 28, 2018. "It's almost like a puzzle because the words make sense for the original context as well," said Chu. "If you took the movie away and you read the doctor's journal entry, you'd be like, 'Okay, yeah, that still reads like a believable set of notes that Dr. Winston would leave about a subject.'"

The visuals in the film are constructed like little puzzle boxes themselves, with numerous Easter eggs that further connect Wrecking Ball to the Overwatch universe and provide additional information about two key locations: Horizon Lunar Colony and Junkertown.

The first shot, for example, depicts an uprising of the genetically modified animals on the colony, painting a dark picture of the facility that challenges the utopian vision described by Winston in "Recall."

Then, in the Scrapyard arena at the end of the film, a very Junkrat-like silhouette appears in the crowd, and the film delivers a distant first look at the Junker Queen, a Wastelander who rose to become the leader of the Junkers.

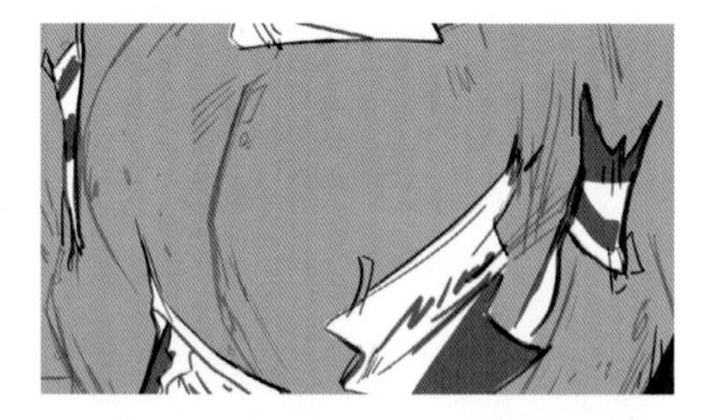

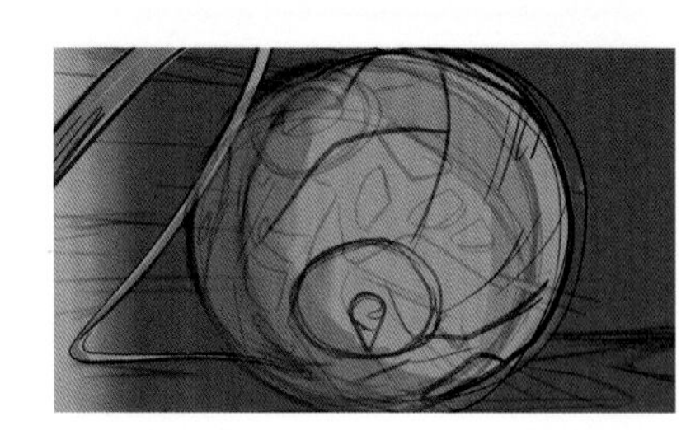

**THESE PAGES** Storyboards representing discarded ideas for how to introduce Wrecking Ball.

## PANNING

▲ The origin story format is economical—it delivers a lot of information in a short period of time. A great motif that the filmmakers developed to support this approach is a long panning shot over a wide image that contains various smaller scenes. "We like to whittle things down. It's like, 'I don't think we need that shot,' or 'We're saying the same thing in two shots. Can we combine them into one?' That's where the long panning shots help," said Schauf.

Using this motif required a different approach to illustration compared to straight-on shots with fixed cameras or less complicated camera movements. "When we're thinking about shots that we're going to pan across or zoom into, there are different compositions for that art than you would find in a regular illustration," said Schauf. "When you're thinking about moving cameras, you have to prepare multiple focal points."

"There was a lot of love and hate about this one," said visual development artist Nesskain, speaking of the opening shot of Wrecking Ball's origin—a long pan across the interior of the Horizon Lunar Colony that ends on Hammond and his escape plans. "Everything in the foreground with the hamster was fun to do. But there were a lot of iterations for the three monkeys along the back wall. It was difficult to get everything in. Everything had to be perfect. Every choice had to be the right choice." ▼

**TOP** Illustration from the opening panoramic shot.

**OPPOSITE, BOTTOM LEFT** Early illustration featuring the portrait of Dr. Winston and a young Winston from the Horizon Lunar Colony.

**ABOVE** Sketches blocking out details in the opening shot.

**LEFT** Illustration showing Wrecking Ball being declared the champion of the Scrapyard by the Junker Queen. Junkrat's silhouette appears in the bottom left.

# ASHE

"ASHE'S ORIGIN STORY WAS THE LAST BIG TURNING POINT ON THE 2.5D PIECES TO HOW WE MAKE THEM TODAY."

—NATHAN SCHAUF, FORMER EDITOR

**ONCE IT WAS DECIDED THAT ASHE WOULD BE REVEALED IN** the "Reunion" short and announced as the next playable hero at BlizzCon on November 2, 2018, the Overwatch team knew they needed an origin piece to flesh out her backstory. Time was short, but the team that worked on "Reunion" was excited to tackle the origin piece. "We had a lot of the same storytelling crew, the same editorial crew," said director Jason Hill. "Almost everybody who'd been working so hard on 'Reunion' was able to immediately roll into the origin and keep that same flavor and feel and style."

This continuity in the production team also made Ashe's piece the first origin story that followed a more traditional, linear cinematic development pipeline. "For Ashe, Jason Hill worked with the storyboard team to create storyboards for the script, and the process suddenly went into something more like prerendered cinematics development," said Tsang.

At first, senior storyboard artist Mio Del Rosario, who had boarded "Reunion," wasn't quite clear on how he should apply his craft to the origin story format. "I wasn't sure how we were going to go about it," said Del Rosario. "Like maybe I would just pitch my ideas, and they would pass them on to the actual illustrator who would take them and make them their own? I wasn't really expecting them to paint over my work. But I was really happy that Nesskain was able to use the compositions I made."

**RIGHT** Sketch to establish the focal point of the opening illustration in the Ashe origin story.

## *ABOVE THE MANTEL*

▲ The opening shot of Ashe's origin story includes a few significant details. The first is the rifle that hangs on the mantel above her head. It's a family heirloom and the same modified gun that she uses in the game. The other detail is the family portrait that hangs above the rifle. It includes Ashe's mother and father and their dog. There's no space for their little girl. This sense that Ashe and her parents exist in separate worlds is reinforced by the two slices of birthday cake served to empty chairs. ▼

**THESE PAGES** In-progress and final illustrations for the opening shot.

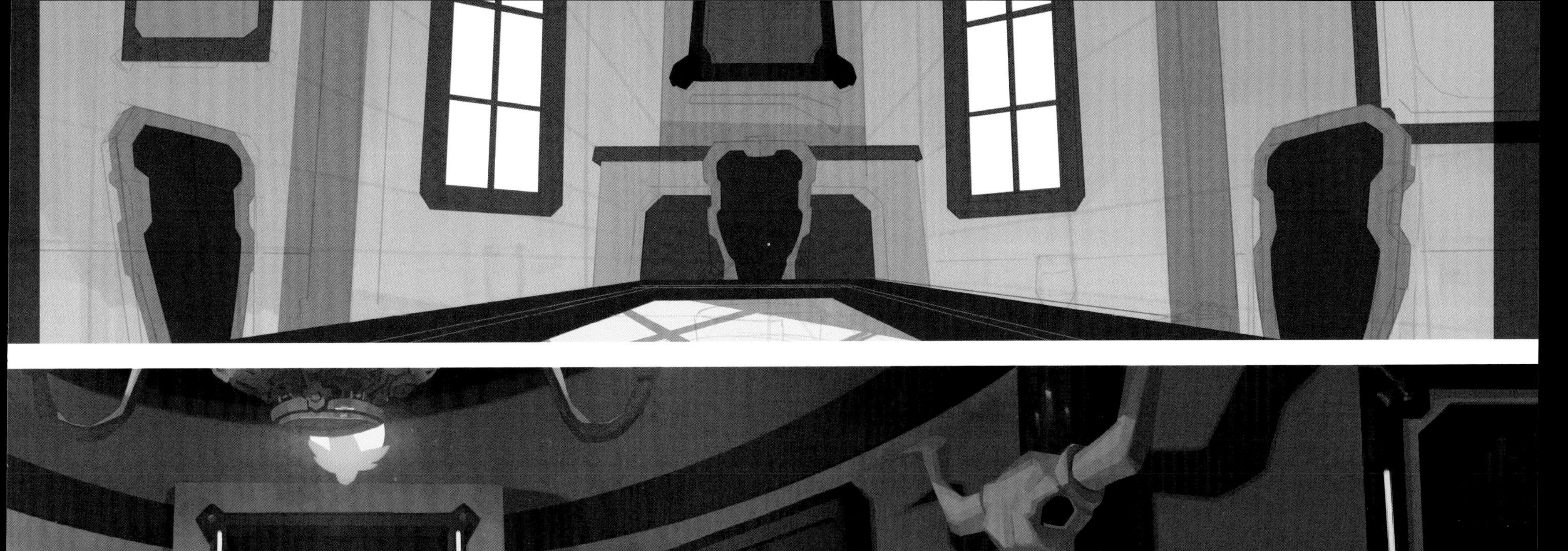

Visual development artist Nesskain was grateful for the leg up since he was in the process of moving from Paris to Irvine, California, to join Blizzard full time. "When I arrived, I had to finish the Ashe piece," he said. "But the storyboards were so well made, it was kind of already done. I didn't want to lose any of the ideas."

Del Rosario had applied the process he uses when working on storyboards for prerendered cinematics to create what he called "schematics" for the final illustrations. "I tried to create beat boards. So instead of imagining a whole sequence, I tried to draw an image that could represent a whole section of the origin piece—like Ashe as a kid, then her as a young adolescent, and then the point where she's in trouble."

One of the beats that Del Rosario found most challenging was the image of young Ashe at her family's dinner table. The filmmakers knew that Ashe came from a rich family and that she was neglected by her parents. "We wanted to make sure that the space was very big to help convey that she's alone," said Del Rosario. "So I thought a lot about architecture but also about how things should be shot. We started with a profile view where we see Ashe walking alone in a hallway. But it was distracting. Instead of seeing Ashe lonely, we just got a cool environment. So Jason told me to make it simple—a straightforward shot of her alone in a big room.

"For each shot, we tried to explore the scenario. And if it didn't feel right or it didn't feel true to the character, then we just omitted it and found an alternative."

This process of working through the details of every shot really impressed *Overwatch*'s character art director, Arnold Tsang, who had kick-started the origin story format with the game's former lead writer, Michael Chu. "The production value really shows on the screen," said Tsang. "It really opened our eyes to what an origin story could be. Now we're using different directors on origin stories, and it's cool to see how their individual styles mesh with the Overwatch universe."

**THIS PAGE** Sketch [top] and final mugshot illustrations [middle and bottom] used in the origin story.

It was always clear that Ashe and B.O.B. have a special relationship; it just wasn't clear where it came from. "The minute we started working on the origin, we knew that it couldn't just be about Ashe," said Hill. "We'd always known that B.O.B. had been around for quite a while, but it wasn't until we really dove into the origin that we were like, 'Oh, yeah, let's make him a robot butler that turns into a bodyguard and friend.'"

If you look closely, the two wanted posters that flank the doors to the jail are for Jeff Chamberlain (left), creative director & vice president of story and franchise development, and Jeff Kaplan (right), *Overwatch*'s game director. The team thought it would be funny for "the two Jeffs" to make their Overwatch debuts as wanted men. Neither Chamberlain nor Kaplan objected.

**THIS PAGE** Sketch (right) and final illustration (bottom) of Ashe leaving a police station, greeted by B.O.B.

### ASHE'S DARK SIDES

▲ Once upon a time, a darker origin story was pitched for Ashe. "It kind of went in a whole different direction, or actually, a couple of different directions," said Schauf. "She was going to be an orphan who grew up in a rival motorcycle gang. Her parents were killed, and the leader of that rival gang was a strong woman who took Ashe under her wing. The idea of her being an orphan kind of stuck since she became this rich kid who was ignored by her parents."

Even after the main features of Ashe's background were solidified, the filmmakers debated how dark they wanted to make her. "She's a rebel, but I wanted to make sure that I didn't depict her like a villain," said Del Rosario.

Skirting this line between rebel and villain led the filmmakers to cut a working illustration of Ashe burning her parents' house down, which the filmmakers thought projected the wrong tone. In the final version, the image was replaced with Ashe leaving a police station. "Some people were like, 'Are her parents in there? Did she kill her parents?'" said Schauf of the house-fire shot. "People could infer that she killed her parents. We really didn't want kids thinking that." ▼

**ABOVE** Illustration of Ashe holding dynamite.

**RIGHT** Sketch for a never-developed illustration showing Ashe leaving her parents' house, which she set on fire.

# BAPTISTE

"THE HOOK WAS 'HOW DOES SOMEONE GO TO THE DARK SIDE?' LIKE, 'HOW DOES SOMEBODY END UP WITH THE WRONG CREW?'"

—JERAMIAH JOHNSON, DIRECTOR

**NOT EVERY HERO'S JOURNEY FOLLOWS A CLEAR TRAJECTORY.** In the case of Baptiste, his was a conscious, hard choice to use his talents for good by separating from Talon, one of the villainous organizations in the Overwatch universe. But the Overwatch team didn't want to reduce Baptiste's story—released on February 25, 2019—simply to one of switching sides. They had to explain how he had gotten mixed up with Talon in the first place—and what made him decide to change the course of his life.

"For Baptiste, it was about creating a certain amount of empathy," said director Jeramiah Johnson. "How did somebody end up one of the bad guys? We just explored that truth."

It had been established early on that Baptiste is an orphan of the Omnic Crisis—one of thirty million who lost their parents during the conflict. That childhood trauma seemed like a good place to start, but it was also incredibly ambitious since it would mean depicting decades of biography in a film that had to be less than two minutes long. "It became, 'Well, how do we tell this?' Or 'What part should we focus on in the telling of this?' Like, 'What are the important bits?'" said Johnson.

**RIGHT** Sketch for the opening illustration of the Baptiste origin story, which pictures Baptiste as a child.

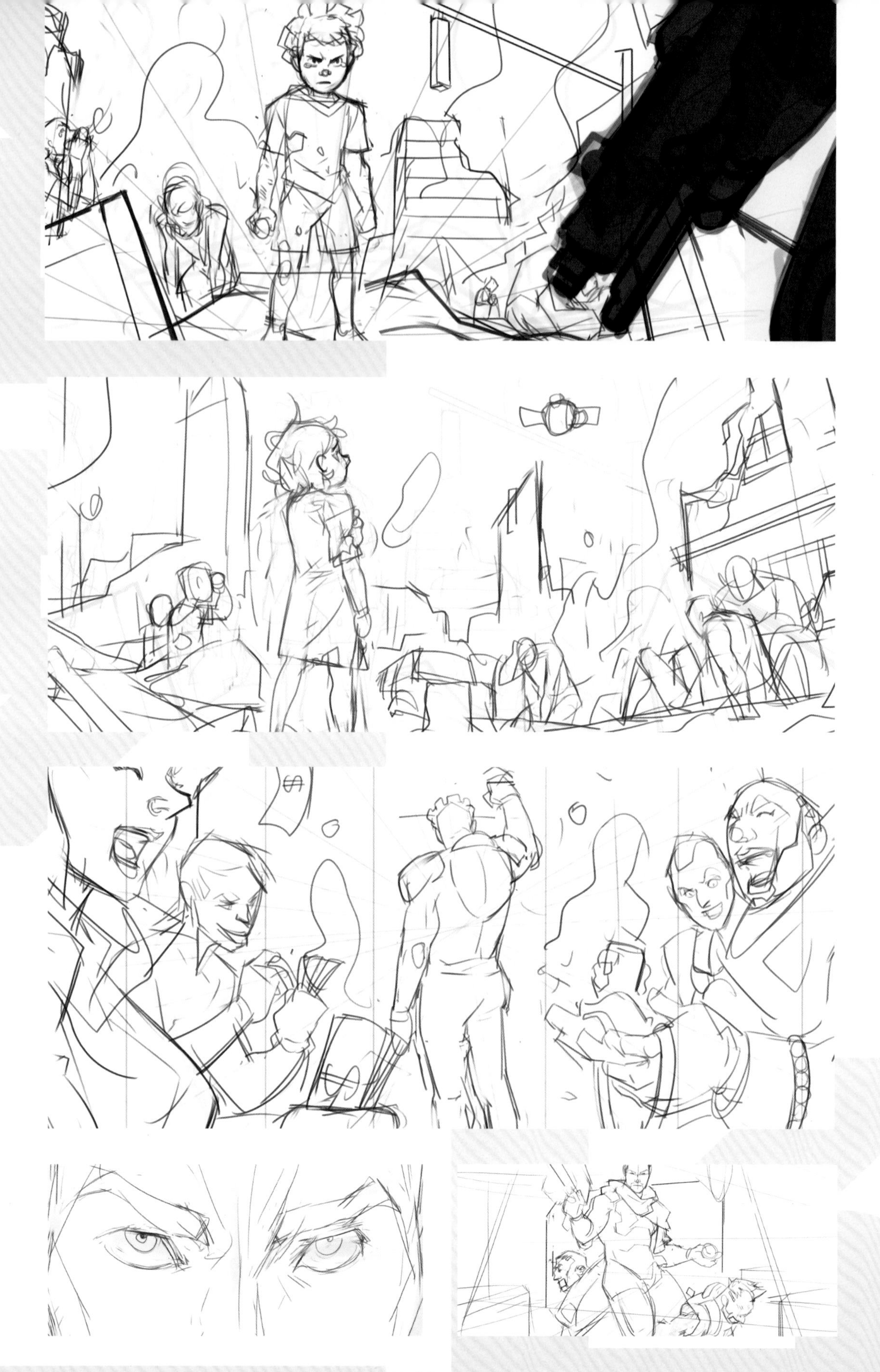

Besides being very selective about the moments they wanted to show, the team also explored playing with the juxtaposition of sound and imagery. What resulted is a powerful assertion of Baptiste's interpretation of some of his life's most significant events. "So you're seeing one thing, you're seeing that struggle, and then you're hearing what he's saying over it," said Johnson. "And you're like, 'Okay, I get this guy. I get where he's coming from.'"

Baptiste sees his life through the lens of choices—choices that he made even if they didn't feel like choices at the time. "He's saying at the beginning, 'I didn't have a choice,' like, 'That choice was taken from me,'" said Johnson. "And then in the second panel, he's like, 'If you wanted to survive, you did what you had to do.' Again, it doesn't feel like a choice. And then he's like, 'If you wanted to change your station in life, you took a hand from whoever gave it to you.' And then he owns it. And he's like, 'You know what the truth is? I had choices all along the way.'"

Until Baptiste shares this revelation, the piece progresses from brightness to darkness, paralleling his descent into the evil represented by Talon. "So it's his path to darkness," said Johnson. "The first shot is the brightest, the second shot is cloudy and you're on a battlefield, and then you're in red and then it's nighttime. And then *boom*, it's bright when he finally makes the turn."

**THIS PAGE** Sketches exploring key moments in Baptiste's origin story.

**OPPOSITE** Final illustrations from the origin piece.

R

**BELOW LEFT & BELOW RIGHT** In-progress versions of Talon armor from the origin story.

**BOTTOM & OPPOSITE** In-progress (bottom) and final illustration (opposite) of Baptiste donning a Talon helmet for the first time.

## *SNAPPING OUT OF IT*

▲ Besides color, another device the filmmakers used to show Baptiste's changing perspective is camera movement. Throughout the piece, the camera starts each shot close-up on Baptiste, tracking out at a steady pace as he talks over the scene, revealing more of what is in the foreground and literally filling in the picture for the audience.

"We repeat the same thing visually because he's doing the same thing to himself over and over again—he's still lying to himself," said Johnson. "Repeating that move over and over again created this rhythm that got you into his cadence of talking, the way he chose to tell his story."

The last shot breaks this cycle while resonating with it. The composition starts even closer-up than the others, framing Baptiste's eyes. And rather than a slow track out, there is an abrupt movement of the camera backward, revealing present-day Baptiste with his helmet removed, clutching a gun and a medical kit with three Talon soldiers tied up at his feet. He's in control, and he finally owns the fact that his life is the result of choices he has made. "We made it a little bit jarring because that's where he's snapped out of it," said Johnson. ▼

**THESE PAGES** Final illustrations from the last shot in the film, which zooms out quickly from a close-up of Baptiste's eyes (above) to a wide shot of him and his surroundings (right).

# SIGMA

"I THINK THE BEAUTY OF THIS PIECE IS THAT WE WERE EXTREMELY LIMITED IN THE NUMBER OF ILLUSTRATIONS WE COULD CREATE. AND AS A RESULT OF THAT RESTRICTION, THE STORY BECAME WHAT IT IS."

—JEFF CHAMBERLAIN, CREATIVE DIRECTOR & VICE PRESIDENT OF STORY AND FRANCHISE DEVELOPMENT

**SIGMA'S ORIGIN STORY—RELEASED ON JULY 22, 2019—** was especially challenging for a number of reasons. Not only does Sigma have a complex relationship with himself (he's severely dissociated), making it difficult for him to tell his own story, but the Overwatch team had an incredibly aggressive schedule that limited the visual development artist, Nesskain, to painting just four illustrations for the piece.

"We talked a lot about who this character is and what the backstory could be, but we always had this lingering thought: 'How are we going to tell this with four images?'" said creative director & vice president of story and franchise development Jeff Chamberlain. "And I remember distinctly that Jeramiah [Johnson, the director] said something like, 'I think I have an idea, but I don't know how to explain it. Let me go figure it out.'"

"Usually, we're doing this very linear storytelling approach, like, this is them in the past, this is them now—that sort of thing. For Sigma, we were like, 'Well, okay, what if we just give the audience the experience rather than telling them what the experience was?'" said Johnson. "So we had this idea, if we just did four paintings, to remix those paintings so that four paintings becomes eight or ten images."

**RIGHT** Sketch of Sigma conducting an experiment in his origin story.

**THIS PAGE** Early storyboards blocking out key moments in the film.

**OPPOSITE** In-progress illustration of Sigma conducting an experiment (top) and the final illustration from the film (bottom).

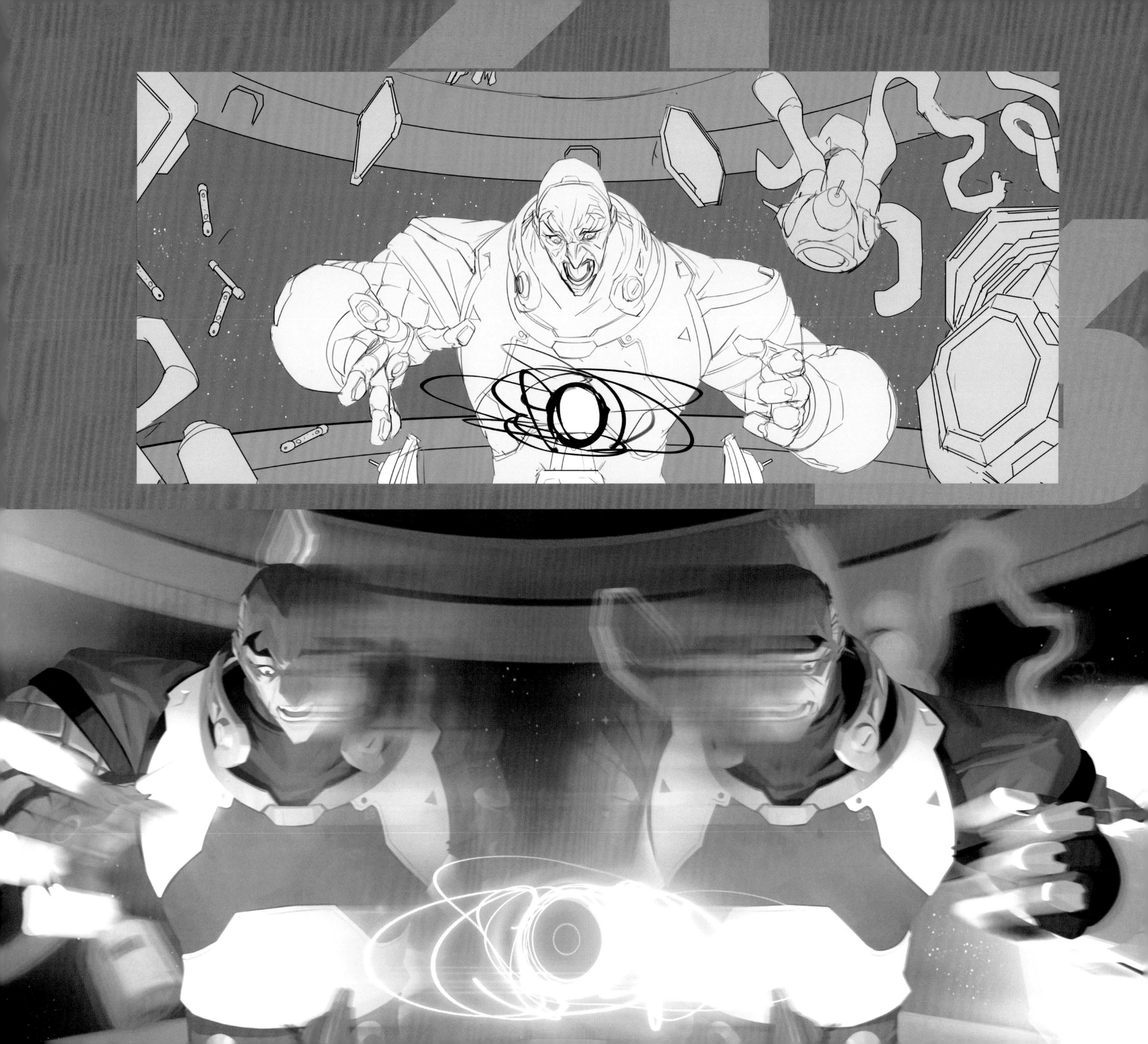

Working closely with Nesskain and editor Michael Bancroft, Johnson was able to develop the idea into a rough animatic that he showed to the rest of the Overwatch team. The demonstration started with Sigma shot straight-on in different poses against backgrounds that correlate with the chosen stances. Then each portrait is lifted and set against mismatched backgrounds, creating a sense of dislocation and disorientation. This technique turned the limited number of illustrations into a storytelling device that expresses the addled mindset of the character.

"Jeramiah came back with an animatic that was fairly detailed and accurate to what it is today," said Chamberlain. "He just played it, and it was one of those moments where you're like, 'Oh, okay, that's exactly what it should be.'"

Kicking off formal production, Johnson asked principal writer Andrew Robinson to write multiple vignettes that could be remixed with the illustrations as opposed to one script. "I was like, Andrew, write what he's feeling at a certain period of time, what he's dealing with during that period of time, and we'll just find it in the edit," said Johnson.

In the editing room, Johnson and Bancroft experimented with pacing to play with the audience. "We wanted to have a slow start, where it seemed like it would maybe be a normal origin story," said Johnson. "Sigma's talking about himself, an idea he cares about. And then all of a sudden, it just goes off the rails, and you're like, 'Wait, what?' And from that moment, everybody's leaning in.

"Sigma was kind of a case study in keeping the audience from not getting comfortable. Because it's really easy, if something is linear, to start to predict what's happening. But when something is nonlinear, it can be unexpected. And I think that that was the success of it."

**TOP LEFT, MIDDLE LEFT, BOTTOM LEFT** In-progress illustration (middle) exploring how to layer mathematical equations (bottom) into a final image in the film (top).

**TOP RIGHT** Concept of the medical identification tag worn by Sigma.

**OPPOSITE** Final illustrations from the film.

R
E
a
f²/Gmₚ² ≅ -α/(1+α)

## SIGMA, EXPLAINED

▲ Sigma was championed early on by *Overwatch*'s game director, Jeff Kaplan, but the character was difficult for many people to grasp. "I kept saying, 'I don't want this to just be a character who is insane.' That's not who Sigma is," said Kaplan. "The type of character that I wanted him to be is not crazy; he's dissociated—he literally thinks he's living in a different space and time. To me, it was very obvious how this was different from him just being mentally insane."

This gap in understanding led to lots of concepts that drew on familiar mad-scientist tropes, which didn't hit the mark for Kaplan. "I felt like people didn't get it," he said. "I understood who I wanted this character to be. But it wasn't clear to other people.

"And we took this leap of faith where we ended up saying to Jeramiah, 'Just show us your idea.' And I remember, after seeing a rough version of the movie, I never had to explain Sigma to anybody ever again. Like, the movie did such a good job of capturing the character, the character didn't require any further explanation." ▼

**RIGHT** Illustration from the end of the piece, which shows Sigma as part of Talon.

# ECHO

"THERE ARE SO MANY CHARACTERS THAT HAVE BEEN SEEDED IN OVERWATCH. IT'S JUST A MATTER OF, 'WHEN IS THE RIGHT TIME TO GROW EACH CHARACTER?'"

—DOUG GREGORY, DIRECTOR

**INSPIRED BY THE SUCCESS OF THE SIGMA ORIGIN STORY,** the Overwatch team saw Echo's origin—released on March 18, 2020—as an opportunity to push the boundaries of the motion-story medium. "We were pushing 2.5D into 3D," said producer Emily Hsu. "We actually tricked a few people in the studio. They were so surprised, they asked, 'When did we start doing origin stories in 3D?'"

The film feels 3D because of its defining 360-degree "bullet time" effect. Dr. Mina Liao, Echo's creator, is spun around in slow motion as she experiences the last moment of her life. The camera rotates around the character, giving the viewer glimpses into shards of glass that reflect her memories, before Mina finally dies and her greatest gift to the world, Echo, activates. "When you see your life flash before your eyes as you're dying, you're capturing an entire lifetime," said director Doug Gregory. "We wanted to capture an eternity in a moment. Bullet time seemed like a great way to do it."

To achieve the orbital effect, Gregory consulted with motion-story supervisor Matthew Mead, who quickly put together a rough layout that showed how he could pull off the shot if he could get three paintings from different angles.

**RIGHT** In-progress illustration of Echo from her origin story.

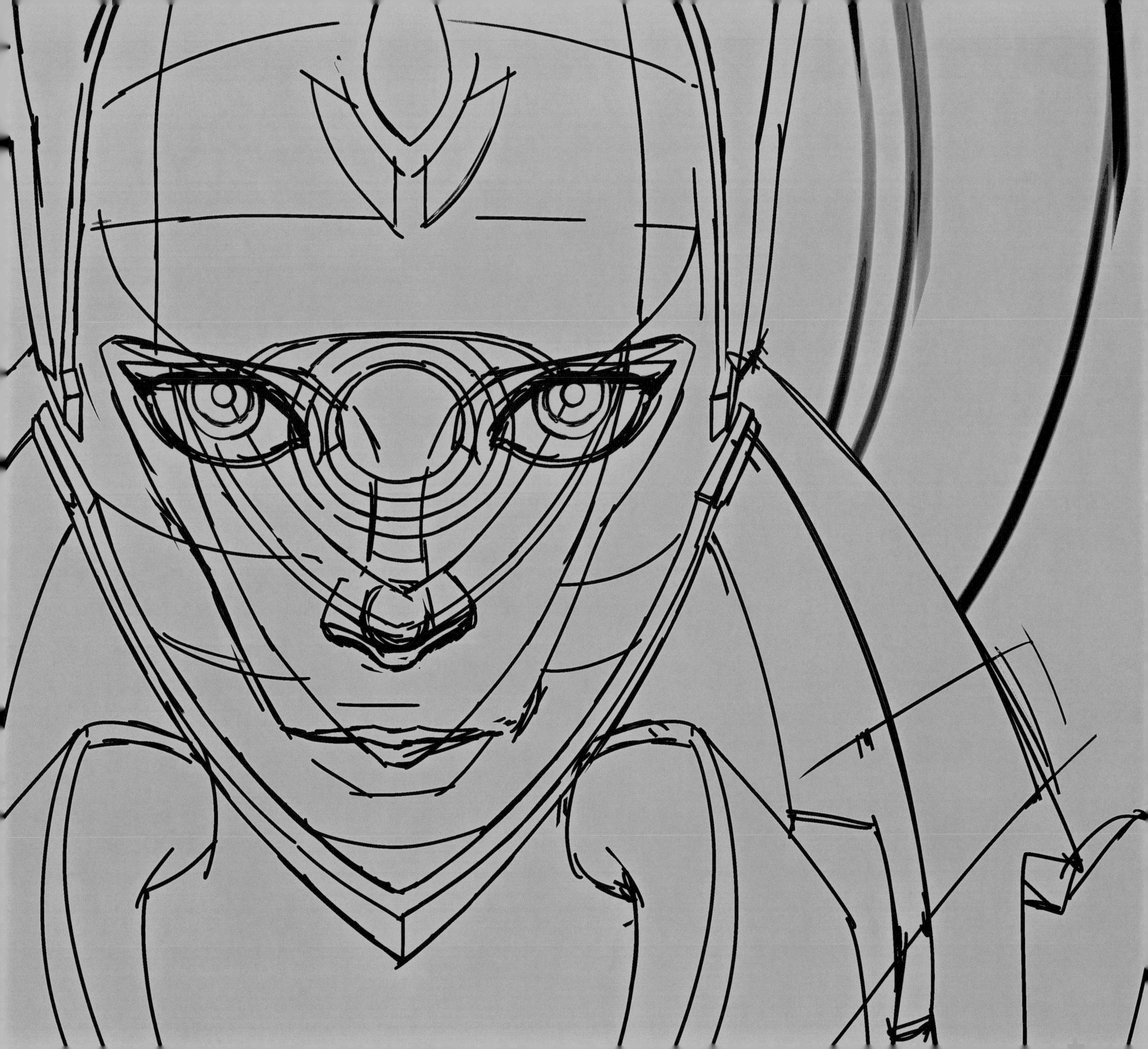

Layered onto that was the idea of shards of glass containing some of Dr. Liao's memories. The first shard shows her joining the Omnica Corporation, where she led the research-and-development team, discovering the next generation of omnics. The second moment shows her being invited by Jack Morrison to help during the Omnic Crisis—an invitation that would lead to her joining Overwatch. Finally, the last shard shows her working on Echo, her life's work.

To pull together this story that jumps between moments in time, the filmmakers had to work in an iterative, nonlinear fashion. During the weeks the show was in production, the team met regularly to collaborate across disciplines and refine the vision. "We would do quick storyboards for it, Nesskain would draw a couple of things that we would put in a very loose edit," said Gregory. "As soon as we started getting the timing of the pictures, we could tell if there was too much dialogue. Then it became, 'Well, let's make this sentence a little shorter because it gives us a better rhythm for the whole piece.' So it was a very back-and-forth process."

**THIS PAGE** Sketches (left) and color illustrations (right) of Dr. Liao suspended in midair after an explosion.

Dr. Liao and Echo have their own unique dynamic as the presence of the latter emerges just as the former expires. "Mina has a sense of extreme responsibility for Echo, as well as a sense of hope for what she might achieve," said senior writer Robert Brooks. "But rather than seeing their relationship as that of a mother and her child, which is probably a perfectly valid view, I approached it as though a skilled mentor were training an apprentice with extraordinary potential. Mina always hoped Echo would be able to achieve greater things than she could alone. Mina's tragedy is that she never got to see if she was right."

The film ends with this ambiguity regarding Echo's character. When she awakens in the final shot, the camera faces her straight on in close-up, her expression inscrutable. "I decided to make her a little cold because she was sleeping," said visual development artist, Nesskain. "Her expression is a blank with a straight line for a mouth—no smile, nothing. She's waking up. That's why I wanted to keep it neutral."

**TOP LEFT** Storyboards depicting the zoom in on Echo in the final shot of the origin piece.

**TOP RIGHT** Sketch of Echo, dormant.

**BOTTOM RIGHT** Final illustration of Echo close up, activated.

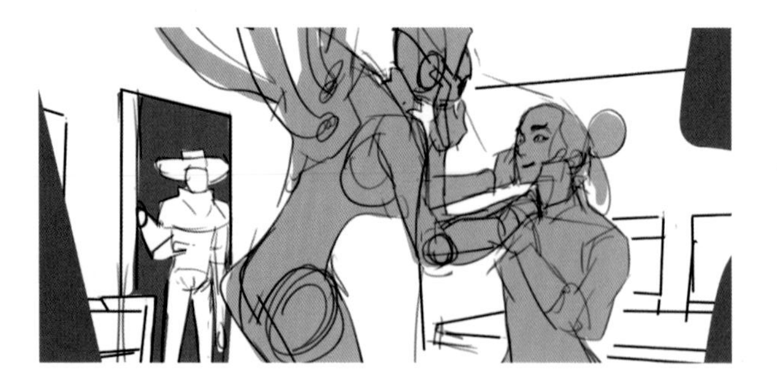

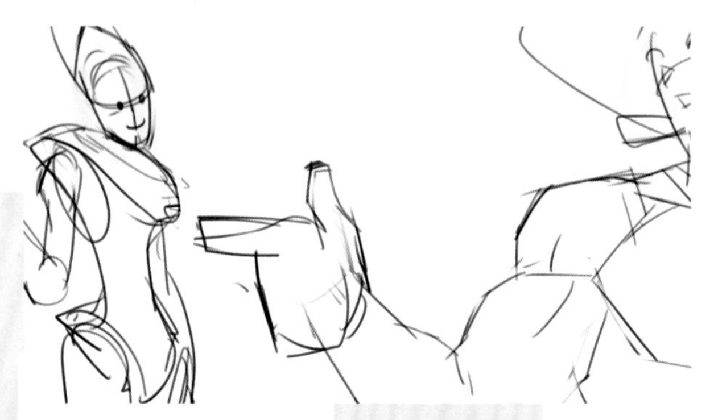

## DEFINING DR. LIAO

▲ Dr. Liao, one of the artificial intelligence researchers who invented omnics, is a character who has existed in Overwatch lore since the beginning. But until Echo's origin piece, she hadn't been depicted in an official Overwatch cinematic. "There was some art here and there for her," said Gregory. "But she wasn't a concrete thing."

Fortunately, Nesskain was able to nail her look early on in the film's development process, which was crucial. "There were a couple of small iterations to her eyes and nose, but they were minor tweaks, which was great for our production schedule because she provided the framework for the whole piece," said Hsu.

As far as Dr. Liao's backstory was concerned, the team wanted to make sure to outline where she fit in with Overwatch, the organization, thereby explaining Echo's connection to the group. Initially, the thought was to include McCree—who is reunited with Echo in "Reunion"—and Torbjörn. "Torbjörn doesn't like omnics or AI in general, so we thought about showing him as Mina's outspoken critic," said Brooks. "McCree was the opposite. He was one of Mina's most valued friends who had no doubts about Echo's importance and was willing to do anything to make sure her legacy wasn't forgotten."

But introducing Dr. Liao and Echo as sources of controversy within Overwatch didn't feel right. "The problem was simple: it made Echo feel incredibly sinister, like she might be a doomsday AI just waiting to take over the planet. It even came close to implying that Mina designed her that way," said Brooks. "That isn't how we view either Mina or Echo. By focusing on Mina's hopes and regrets instead, we left no doubt about her intentions: she wanted Echo to be a force for good." ▼

**OPPOSITE, TOP LEFT** Storyboards exploring how McCree might have interacted with Dr. Liao and Echo.

**OPPOSITE, MIDDLE LEFT & BOTTOM RIGHT** Storyboards exploring how the Bastion units and Torbjörn might have had contact with Dr. Liao.

**OPPOSITE, BOTTOM LEFT** Final illustration of Jack Morrison asking Dr. Liao to join Overwatch.

**THIS PAGE** Sketch (right) and final illustration (below) of Dr. Liao inspecting omnics in production.

**LEFT** Final illustration of Dr. Liao admiring her life's work, Echo.

# IN-GAME CINEMATICS

FOUR

**WHEN BLIZZARD FIRST STARTED MAKING CINEMATICS FOR OVERWATCH, THEY WERE COMPLETELY SEPARATE FROM THE GAME. THEY HELPED ESTABLISH THE UNIVERSE** and the characters, but they weren't woven directly into the gameplay.

Looking forward to *Overwatch 2*, where in-game cinematics (IGCs) are an integral part of the gaming experience, the Overwatch team knew they needed to build an IGC pipeline to incorporate visual storytelling into PvE missions and events. To do so, they took a test-and-learn approach, where they experimented with formats for delivering content and gauged how far they could push the game engine in terms of animation, lighting, and rendering.

The first cinematic tied to an in-game mission. "Uprising" wasn't made using the game engine; instead, it exploited the flexible 2.5D format used for the origin stories. With "Junkertown: The Plan," though, the team moved toward true IGC production using the 3D game engine.

LEFT In-progress illustration for the final shot in the 2.5D motion story that introduces the Archives event, "Uprising."

This approach has a couple of key advantages when it comes to bringing cinematics and the game closer together. The first is that it allows the filmmakers to use game assets with minimal alterations. "You can leverage characters, existing environments, effects," said former producer Rachel Richmond. "So the visual translation between gameplay and cinematic is as seamless as possible; you're not really breaking with the player's experience."

The other advantage of using the game engine is that it allows for faster, more iterative rendering and review so that the transition between the cinematic and gameplay can be matched up more quickly. "What is great is that we can put cinematic work in progress in a rough version of a mission and play it," said Richmond. "So the people working on the game can experience it and ask, 'So how does this line up with the gameplay we're creating?' And that generates so much vital feedback. Because what works as a cinematic just by itself might not work when connected to gameplay.

"We knew when we were working on these mission events we were going to have to change our way of thinking. There was a very different collaborative energy. We had never really done something like this before in quite the same way."

**ABOVE** Sketch of the groundbreaking depicted at the beginning of the 2.5D motion-story introduction to "Uprising."

**RIGHT** Storyboard of Junkrat and Roadhog running, from the in-game cinematic "Junkertown: The Plan."

## MASTERING THE HANDOFF

One of the most difficult challenges for the team to overcome was how to make the transitions between cinematics and gameplay feel as seamless as possible. "Ultimately, the cinematic needs to get you excited about getting to the gameplay," said Jason Hill, who directed all the IGCs that hook up directly with gameplay. "We know the gameplay needs to start at a certain spot, the spawn zone, meaning we need to get you as close as possible so the handoff to begin the gameplay feels organic. We build the cinematic and the game at the same time and work collaboratively to sync up all those points where the cinematic stops and the gameplay starts."

"It's really a question of how we support these missions," said Richmond. "We want to make sure that we hook people and that the time they spend watching the cinematics feels exciting and engaging and fruitful. And then they are so amped by the time that it's done. You know, they are so excited to play this game!"



**TOP LEFT** Illustration featured in the 2.5D motion story outro for the "Retribution" Archives event.

**RIGHT** Overwatch recruitment poster created for the "Uprising" event.

# UPRISING

"IT COULD BE THE BEGINNING OF A NEW WAR BETWEEN HUMANS AND OMNICS . . . UNLESS WE CAN STOP THEM!"

—TRACER

THE "UPRISING" CINEMATIC WAS MADE FOR THE FIRST Overwatch Archives event on April 11, 2017. Although it didn't feature the 3D assets of a true IGC, the short was a crucial step toward telling stories in the game. The team used "Uprising" to experiment with how they could deliver an engaging narrative and provide important context for the game mission. "One thing that we realized when playing the mission early on is that you really needed a story intro to understand what was going on," said *Overwatch*'s former lead writer Michael Chu. "Having the experience making the origin movies, we knew it was an efficient way to do a bunch of world building. With a couple images, we could really show different parts of what was happening."

When it comes to world building, "Uprising" was geared toward introducing a faction that would become increasingly important in the Overwatch story: Null Sector. "When we tell these stories, we're thinking about how people are experiencing the overall narrative of Overwatch," said Chu. "We've known for a long time what direction the universe is going, and we decide when we should sprinkle in some things that seed stuff that's coming in the future. Having Null Sector in 'Uprising' is a great example because we knew that this was a villain for the future, and we wanted a cool way to show them off for the first time."

**RIGHT** Final illustration of an omnic protecting humans from Null Sector pursuers in the "Uprising" 2.5D motion story introduction.

ROBOTROPOLIS
A CITY OF HARMONY..

"Uprising" also cleaved to the origin story format in that it was told from a character's point of view. "I think the first draft I ever wrote was more of a Jack Morrison narration like, 'Hey, here's what you're going to do,'" said Chu. "But it felt like a missed opportunity to do more than just have someone explain what was happening. So we chose to do it in Tracer's voice, so not only are you finding out what's going on, you're getting it from the point of view of someone who has just joined Overwatch. That's one of the main features of the origin movies—that they're all from a specific point of view."

The same team that was working on the origin stories at the time also worked on the "Uprising" cinematic, which followed a similar development process. visual development artist Nesskain provided the illustrations, applying his signature use of color.

One of the things the creators wanted to emphasize was how camera movements could contribute to the emotional tenor of the film. Since "Uprising" is a story of the accepted social order falling apart, it made sense for the camera to move in different directions during each shot, creating a feeling of unease, disruption, and a fundamental lack of resolution.

In the first shot, the camera moves left to right, reinforcing the idea that progress is being made when it comes to human-omnic relations. Then, in the second shot, which depicts the attack on King's Row, the camera reverses course, moving right to left. "It's like all the good that we were building between humans and omnics—*Boom*!—now we're going in the other direction," said former editor Nathan Schauf, who edited and codirected the piece. "We wanted to contrast everything between them. And then we go back to neutral, where the omnics are protecting humans with a straight-on shot. Then, when we go to the hero shots, we pull out. This was one where I was like, 'Every camera move has to be different.'"

**OPPOSITE, TOP LEFT** Sketch of an omnic protecting humans from Null Sector pursuers.

**OPPOSITE, MIDDLE & BOTTOM** Evolution from sketch (middle left) to more developed layout (middle right) to color illustration (bottom).

**THIS PAGE** Overwatch recruitment posters made for the "Uprising" Archives event.

## MAP EFFECTS

▲ Like all cinematics tied to an in-game mission, "Uprising" takes place in a playable map: King's Row. Since the event happens in the past, it prompted the Overwatch team to think through how the location must have looked during the time of "Uprising."

Two of the areas that underwent the most significant changes were the power plant and the train station. "We always imagined the power plant as a place where a lot of the omnics were pushed to live; the humans forced them to live inside the deeper parts of the plant," said *Overwatch*'s assistant art director Dion Rogers. "But in the event version, you get to see the power plant before all the objects were pushed in there."

The train station was edited to allow players to walk from the train they arrive on to the level. "Normally, that train station is just a spawn room," said Rogers. "In the event, you can see the train station as an active place. You get to see it before things went bad.

"When we went back in time, we wanted to show what it was like beforehand, to show the cost of the destruction. You know, 'What did we lose because of this event?' It helped us define King's Row a bit more." ▼

**THESE PAGES** Evolution from sketch (above) to more developed layout (opposite, top) to final illustration (right).

**THESE PAGES** Work-in-progress and final illustrations for the last shot in the 2.5D motion story introduction.

# JUNKERTOWN: THE PLAN

"WELP, THERE'S TWO THINGS THAT SOLVE EVERY PROBLEM: MONEY AND EXPLOSIVES."

—JUNKRAT

WHEN THE OVERWATCH TEAM APPROACHED TERRAN Gregory, who had helped architect Blizzard's IGC pipeline and directed dozens of cinematics for *World of Warcraft*, the ask was twofold: they wanted him to make an IGC to announce the new Junkertown map at Gamescom on August 21, 2017, and they needed him to prove that the *Overwatch* game engine could be used as a platform to produce cinematic content.

"So the initial ask was very simple," said Gregory. "It was just a couple-minute movie to get the audience excited about the new map. That's not a lot of parameters. And it needed to be driven using the game engine. The first step, then, was to take a look at what was going to be available. And at that time, the only thing that we had available was a rough concept of the front gate of Junkertown. So we had a picture of a front gate, and we had two characters, Junkrat and Roadhog. It was almost like one of those improvisation challenges, where you're onstage and they pull two words out of a hat. Challenge accepted!"

RIGHT Early concept of the gate to Junkertown.

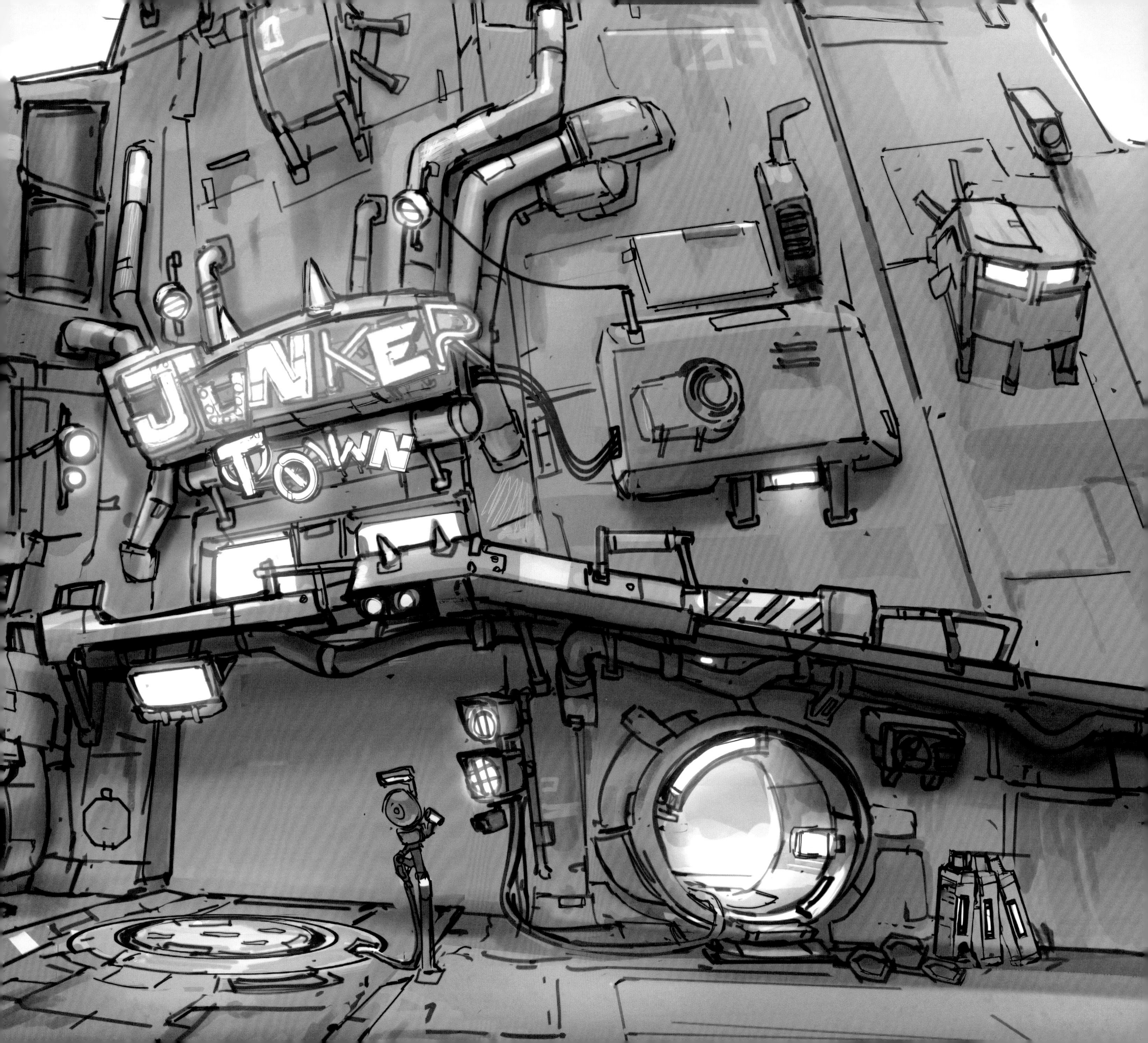
JUNKER
TOWN

Working with just Junkrat, Roadhog, and the gate to Junkertown, the team hatched the idea that Junkrat and Roadhog must be locked out and are trying to get in. "The engine features were still in development, and so we had no choice but to keep the project contained to a small number of locations and characters," said senior writer Robert Brooks. "From the beginning, Terran held a strong vision of Junkrat trying—and failing—to explain his 'brilliant' strategy to his partner in crime, and we stuck with that the entire project."

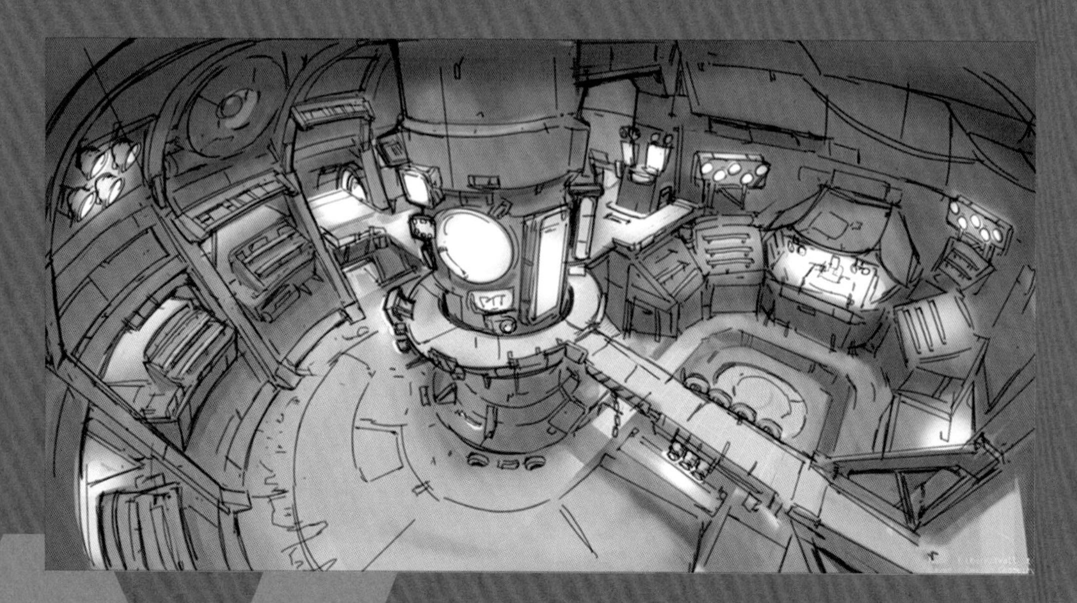

"The plan is deeply flawed. But in Junkrat's mind, it all makes perfect sense," said Gregory. "So we started bouncing ideas back and forth, and we arrived at this idea of an escalating series of moments denying Junkrat what he wants. And so it became a three-stage joke—classic cartoon comedy."

Although Junkrat and Roadhog are humorous characters on the fringes of the core Overwatch aesthetic, the idea of emulating a classic cartoon stretched the boundaries of the world a bit too far. To create a sense of separation that would make the jump into the genre work, the filmmakers added a special intro, much like they had for the Junkrat and Roadhog origin story, "A Moment in Crime Special Report: The Junkers." "The reason we wanted an animated

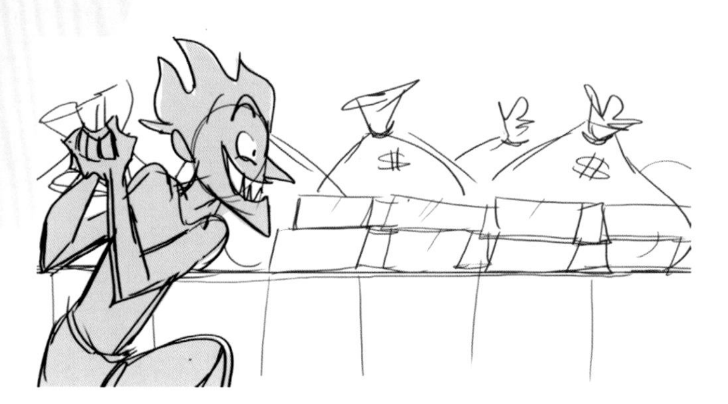

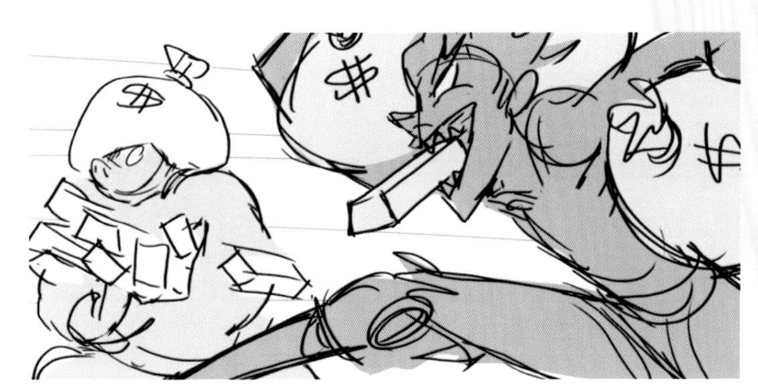

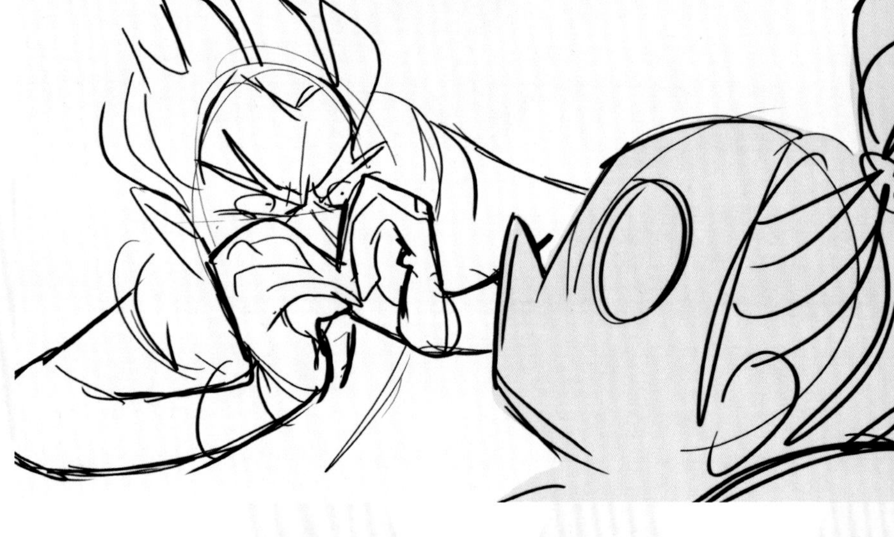

OPPOSITE Junkertown environmental concepts.

THIS PAGE Storyboards exploring Junkrat's expressions and the potential for physical comedy.

intro title sequence was to create this sense of like, 'Oh, this is more like if a cartoon was made about Overwatch and less a day in the life of the characters,'' said Gregory.

As the day approached when the filmmakers would need to pitch their idea to the rest of the team, Gregory started to get a little nervous. Had they gone too far? But there was no going back. "The madness took us, as it does, and it was just fun," he said. "It was too much fun to get into the head of Junkrat. And then it was the day. Jeff Kaplan, Michael Chu, and some other people from the team came to the meeting, and I got in front of them. And this was not like, 'Let's read a script.' I acted out the whole short, voices and all."

"It was like a one-man drama," said *Overwatch*'s game director, Jeff Kaplan. "Terran acted out the entirety of what we know today as 'The Plan.' It was the most entertaining pitch I've ever seen. Usually when people pitch things, they'll pitch maybe the beat boards, or they'll describe certain scenes, and it's always exciting. But Terran literally acted it out, including singing the theme song exactly as it is in the movie today. It was so fun and so entertaining. So with 'The Plan,' there was never any question what it was going to be like; you had seen the movie already."

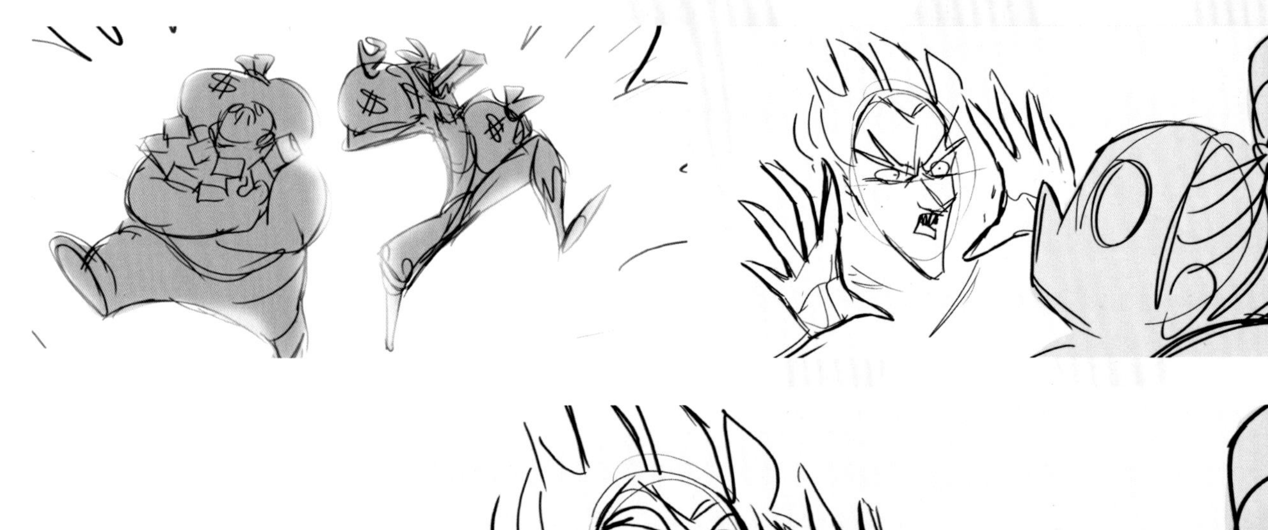

JUNKER
TOWN

## CLASSIC ANIMATION

▲ Junkrat and Roadhog are already two of the most cartoonish characters in Overwatch, both in terms of their sensibility and their appearance. In "Junkertown: The Plan," the filmmakers really wanted to play this up by animating them in a way that was reminiscent of classic animation.

"The movie was staged in line with classic cartoon stylings, as if it was a stage play with flatter compositions," said Gregory. "There are a lot more full-body shots than you'll see in any of the other Overwatch cinematics."

This tendency to favor broader shots gave the animators the opportunity to emphasize expressive, wide-ranging movements and to vary the speed of the action to give it the snappiness of traditional hand-drawn cartoons. "We shot a lot of reference with the audio played back at half speed," said animation supervisor Hunter Grant. "Then we would speed up the video to double speed, giving the reference a much more cartoon-like look."

"The animators, they live to make this stuff," said Gregory. "They grew up watching all manner of cartoons. When you give people who have spent their lives studying this art form the opportunity to work on something like this, they throw themselves into it. Every one of them did—and you can see that through the joy of Junkrat." ▼

**THESE PAGES** Storyboards depicting Junkrat explaining the plan to Roadhog.

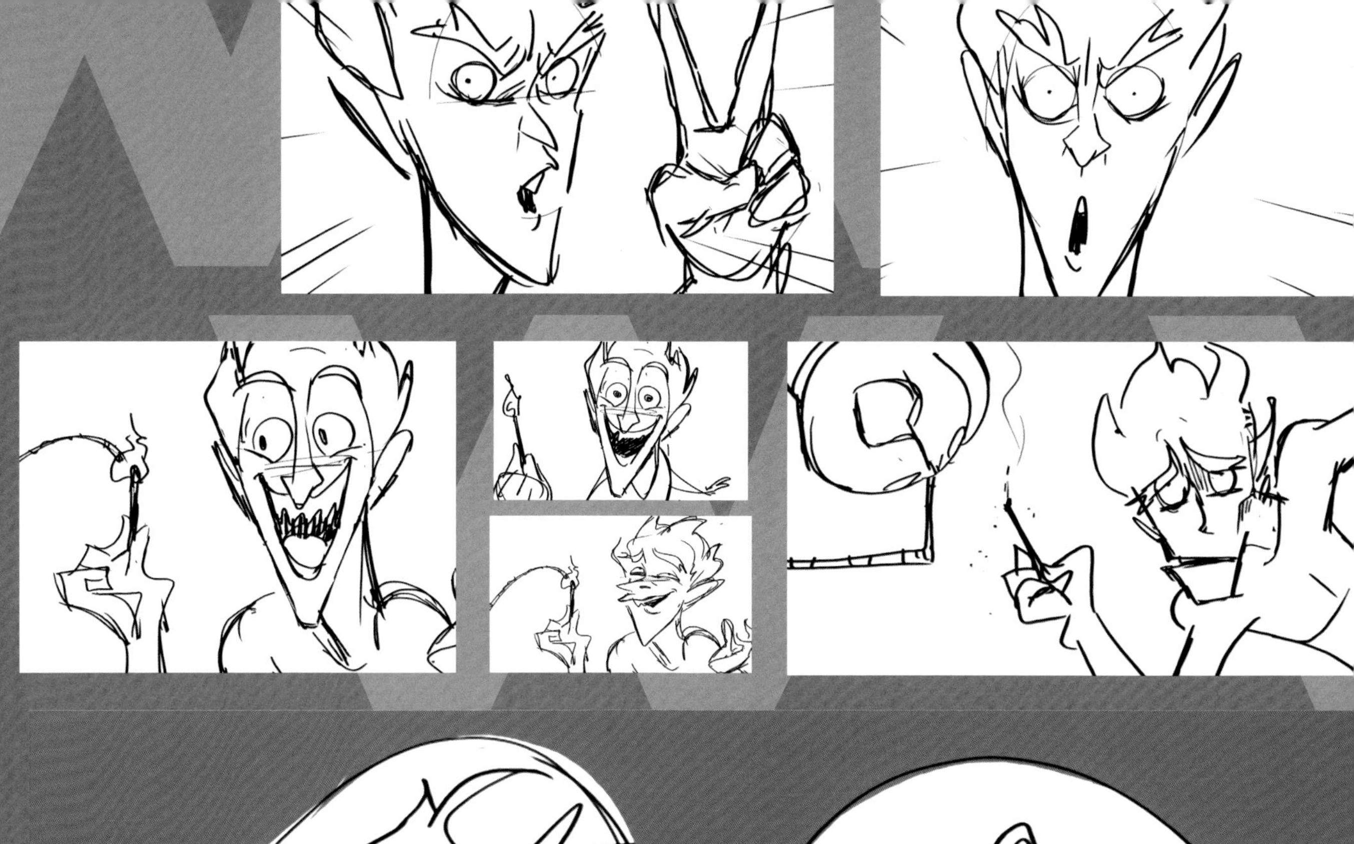

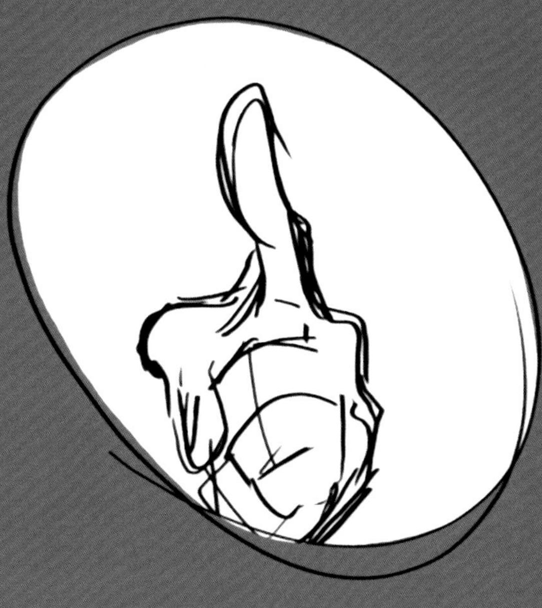

"'The Plan' helped us determine what the final payload was going to look like," said *Overwatch*'s assistant art director, Dion Rogers. "Junkrat and Roadhog have been stealing things from all over the world. So we wanted to show the accumulation of that. But we wanted there to be something off about it. There are these hidden explosives underneath if you look at it carefully. And it's really funny because a lot of players recently discovered this, even though it's been in the game for a while. They started to really study the scene, like 'Oh, this is from the cinematic.'"

**RIGHT** Concepts of the Junkertown payload.

FUE

# RETRIBUTION

"REYES, WHAT DID YOU DO? THIS WAS *NOT* THE PLAN!"

—McCREE

**THE "RETRIBUTION" IN-GAME CINEMATICS—RELEASED ON** April 10, 2018—were tied to the second Archives event, which was the first mission to feature both an intro and an outro cinematic. "So it was kind of like, 'We'll just do this intro cinematic,'" said director Jason Hill. "And then I realized we needed some kind of outro to continue the story."

To tackle both cinematics, the filmmakers decided to adopt the two different styles and production workflows at their disposal. They would make an intro using in-game assets, while the outro would be done in the style of the 2.5D motion stories. "That allowed us to change the framing of how the outro worked. It became McCree's point of view a few weeks later," said Hill.

The intro, though, had to have a much tighter integration with the gameplay since it would lead directly into the Archives event—a Blackwatch mission where the team is supposed to extract a senior member of Talon from a compound in Venice, only to have Gabriel Reyes execute him on-site. Narratively, the cinematic had to explain the details of the mission and how it went wrong. And functionally, it had to deliver the characters to the spawn room in a way that would prepare players to jump right into the action.

**RIGHT** Final illustration from the 2.5D outro to the "Retribution" Archives event.

030
030
220
230

THESE PAGES A mix of in-progress and final renders from the event's in-game cinematic intro.

Finding this perfect synergy was challenging because the game event was being made at the same time as the cinematic. "This is what is really difficult about in-game cinematics," said former producer Rachel Richmond. "There is such a delicate balance between the elements of a cinematic—action, storytelling, pacing—and the elements of gameplay. You have to be so careful and conscious of what is going on in the mission. Is this mission supposed to feel dire? Is it supposed to feel hopeful? What's the dialogue between the characters? And you may not have all of those answers when you start production on your cinematic."

"Retribution" was particularly nuanced because it dealt with a foundational moment in Overwatch history—the moment "when everything may have gone wrong" with Blackwatch, according to McCree. To show McCree's unease with Reyes's leadership—and the jockeying for position between the two heroes—the animators used expressive body language. "In the way McCree addresses Reyes, there's a lot of consideration with how the beats play," said in-game cinematic CG supervisor Jim Jiang. "Like the moment where Reyes shoots the Talon member Antonio—the way McCree has to stand up to Reyes. A lot about their relationship is communicated by how they are posed relative to each other—like they are roughly equal, which makes you wonder who's in charge of the mission."

Genji, another participant in the event, also has a subtle way of communicating using his body, which the filmmakers tweak to perfection. "Genji's funny because he's always cool," said Jiang. "Like, the biggest reaction that we play out with him is he kind of does a head turn. A lot goes into deciding how much his head will turn."

## ANTONIO AND HIS OFFICE

▲ Antonio, the senior Talon member, didn't exist prior to the cinematic, which created an interesting situation for the team. For the first time, they would need to create a character using the in-game engine that wouldn't be featured in the game since Antonio dies before the mission begins.

Antonio's existence—and the Venice setting—also prompted the team to flesh out Talon as an organization. "The idea came up that Talon comes from old money," said *Overwatch*'s assistant art director, Dion Rogers. "Like they've been around longer than people expect. The architecture in Venice worked really well with that idea."

Elaborating what that architecture would look like began with a consideration of Antonio's office, which is also the spawn room for the mission. "Most of the room is designed around the cinematic and that final camera shot so that when the players pick their heroes, it feels connected," said Rogers. "Even the window in the spawn room is broken, where Antonio fell out. It all matches up really nicely with the cinematic." ▼

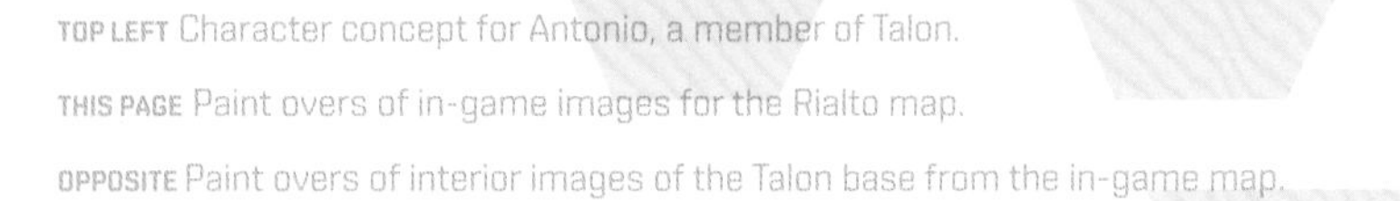

TOP LEFT Character concept for Antonio, a member of Talon.

THIS PAGE Paint overs of in-game images for the Rialto map.

OPPOSITE Paint overs of interior images of the Talon base from the in-game map.

# STORM RISING

"WE'VE WAITED A LONG TIME FOR MAXIMILIEN TO SHOW HIS FACE. IT'S NOW OR NEVER."

—SOJOURN

**THE OVERWATCH TEAM KNEW THAT "STORM RISING"—** released on April 16, 2019—would feature the last in-game cinematics before the announcement of *Overwatch 2*, making it, in many ways, a proving ground for how IGCs would be used in the sequel. This prompted the filmmakers to raise the bar. "For 'Storm Rising,' I specifically let everybody know that we were going to push ourselves on this one," said director Jason Hill.

To start, this meant developing an exciting but outlandish idea and doing everything they could to pull it off. "I remember the day somebody handed me the beat sheet," said former producer Rachel Richmond. "It was like, 'Cut to a car chase.' And I was like, 'All right then, this is going to be a challenge because you can't cut corners. But I also laughed, because it was cool to have something with that complexity in an in-game cinematic. If we could do it, we can do anything. Like we were busting down the doors of what people expect out of an in-game cinematic."

**RIGHT** Final render of Genji slicing a hovercar's wheel off from the in-game cinematic introduction to the "Storm Rising" Archives event.

25

Staging a car chase in an IGC was particularly challenging because car chases cover vast distances, whereas the game environment—which is restricted to the playable map and some of its surroundings—isn't very large. "To make it work, we almost treated it more like a feature film, where they'll rent out a city block to do a car chase, and then they'll redress and then run the same cars down the same street or shoot from different angles so that it feels bigger than it actually is," said Hill.

Even this strategy, however, didn't give the filmmakers enough space to stage an effective car chase at the speeds they envisioned. "We had to build a custom map that was like a kilometer long, which was completely out of scope of what the engine was supposed to do," said in-game cinematic CG supervisor Jim Jiang.

To facilitate this, the environment artists created modular structures that allowed the team to build out as much space as they needed without putting too much strain on the game engine. "We're able to copy them and change their colors and things," said *Overwatch*'s assistant art director, Dion Rogers. "You can extend a street by just copying different sets of buildings. Because the scene goes by so fast with motion blur, you don't see the repetition."

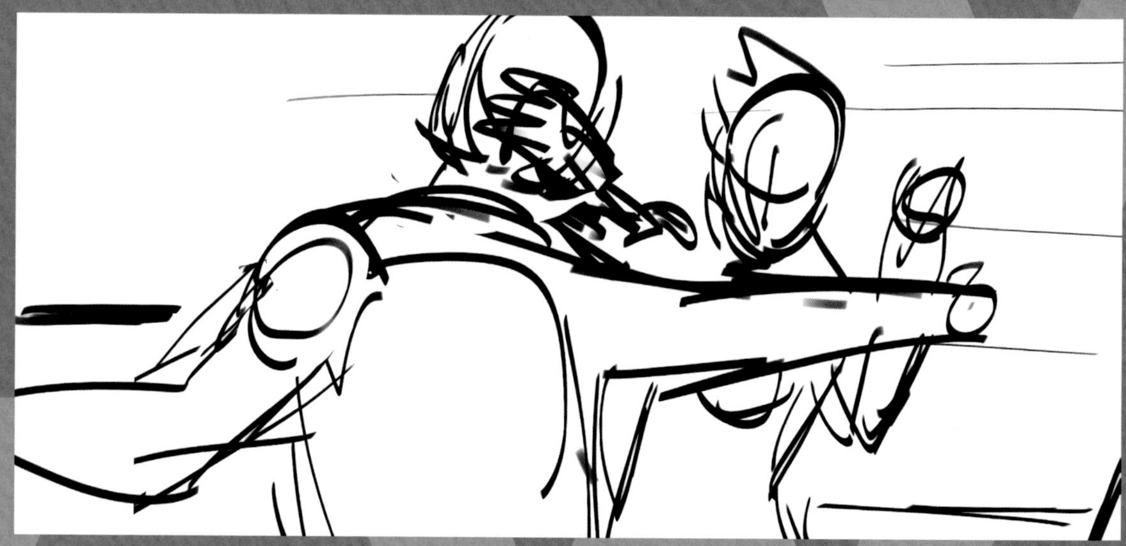

**THIS PAGE** Storyboards exploring the chase during the cinematic introduction.

## *MAX'S EYELIDS*

▲ Maximilien is an omnic who can blink. This isn't typical for omnics, as they don't have eyelids. The filmmakers added them to Max because they needed him to be more expressive, which prompted the question: How did he get them? "He has a little visor that goes over his glowing eyes," said Jiang. "None of the other omnics have that. So that was something that was discussed, like, 'Are omnics going to have eyelids now?' We decided that, no, only Max does because he upgraded."

Making this decision regarding Max's eyelids—as well as establishing his look more generally—was important, as he was supposed to be an integral part of the in-game mission, although his role ended up being limited to the intro and outro cinematics. "He was going to play a bigger role," said Jiang. "The idea was that you're trying to chase him the whole time, but then he didn't make it into the mission. So all the story with Max is purely told in the cinematics." ▼

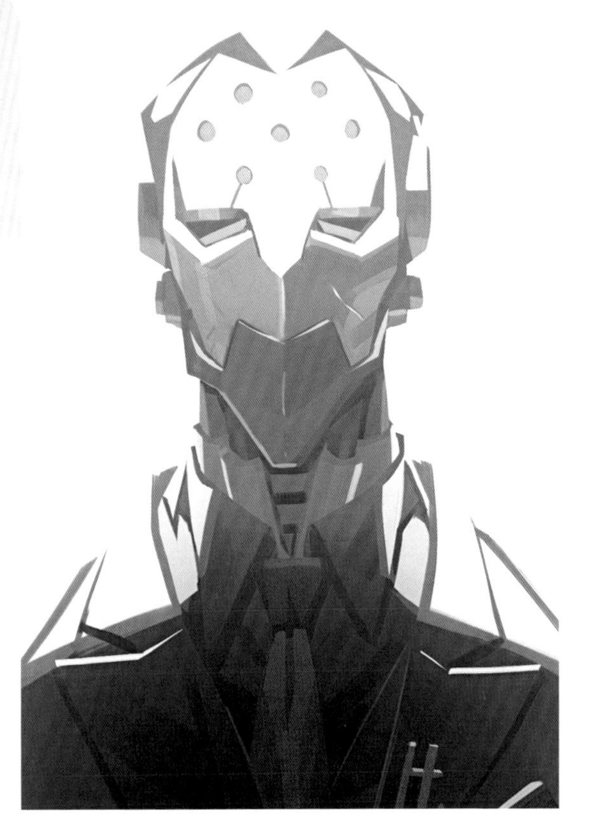

This way of building out the virtual set as needed also affected the film's camera angles and shot durations. "Trying to figure out the scale, we did all these tests," said Jiang. "We did some napkin math and realized, 'Okay, if this shot lasts longer than thirty seconds and they're moving at this speed, they're going to travel three kilometers, and in no way can we fit that in the current map.' We could only do some shots for a second before we'd run out of space. So that put a few constraints on how quickly we had to cut and what angles we were able to use."

Early internal playtests that included the car chase intro were met with feedback from people indicating they wanted to continue the chase in game, which was a sign that the cinematic had exceeded expectations. But it also prompted the team to recalibrate the tone of the IGC and the mission. "We had challenges, I think, because we were so ambitious," said Richmond. "If there is an imbalance in action between the cinematic and the gameplay, you have to figure out how to level them off."

**TOP LEFT** Illustration of Maximilien.

**THIS PAGE** Storyboards featuring Maximilien and Doomfist (top right), and the mysterious omnic who reveals himself at the end of the outro cinematic (middle and bottom).

## TRACER'S BIKE

▲ One question that came up when the filmmakers were contemplating the car chase was why Tracer couldn't just use her Blink ability to intercept the senior Talon member Maximilien, who she and the other heroes are chasing. "In a prerendered cinematic, we might have had her Blink all over the city because it looks cool," said Hill. "But I wanted to keep it more true to the gameplay, where she can only Blink so much before she has to recharge."

This prompted the idea that Tracer chases Max on a hoverbike, which she could use to travel the large distances in the Havana map and then Blink off the bike a few times over short distances, as she does in game. The team's first instinct was to try to repurpose a hoverbike asset from a previous *Overwatch* level. The likely choice was the Route 66 map. "We were like, 'Okay, well, maybe we can take one of these chopper-style bikes and slightly change it and make it feel like it fits," said Hill. "And then, as we started to bring it into the Havana map, it just didn't look right."

"We tried a couple of different substitutions for the bike and then ultimately decided Tracer should have her own motorcycle, like there should be a Tracer motorcycle that fits her character," said Jiang. "I mean, she's a fighter pilot, so of course she rides a motorcycle." ▼

**THIS PAGE** Renders of Tracer's hoverbike.

**OPPOSITE** Renders of the exterior (top) and interior (bottom) of Maximilien's limousine.

## *IN CARS*

▲ Originally, the filmmakers tried to stage the chase using the car models that were already part of the Havana map. But the idea of Talon rolling through the city with a fleet of vintage automobiles didn't cut it. The organization demanded intimidating SUVs, a limo for Max, and the latest car technology. "For Max's limo, we were going to have a limo driver," said Jiang. "We thought it would be funny if an omnic had a human as a driver. But then we decided that the world has self-driving cars. It's the future."

This change, which happened midproduction, gave rise to a funny situation. The limo with the driver had originally been designed with enough interior space to accommodate a front seat. The filmmakers had blocked everything out accordingly. But once the artificial intelligence took over driving, the limo design was shortened since a front seat wasn't needed for a driver. "So we load the asset, and it's way shorter than what we were looking at before," said Jiang. "And we're like, 'Okay, well, the camera won't fit in the car.' We couldn't get the shot that we wanted. It was one of those weird things you don't really think about with CG. You still have to deal with things as if they are physical objects, to a certain extent." ▼

**RIGHT** Final render from the in-game cinematic introduction.

# STOP-MOTION

FIVE

**STOP-MOTION ANIMATION MAY SEEM LIKE A STRANGE MEDIUM TO USE TO DEPICT AN ENTIRELY COMPUTER-GENERATED WORLD, BUT THE TECHNIQUE INHERENTLY** reinforces one of Overwatch's core aesthetic pillars: art that feels handcrafted. "You see evidence of the tangible, real world in stop-motion but also the craftsmanship that goes into it," said producer Emily Hsu, who worked on the two official Overwatch stop-motion animation pieces, "Trace & Bake" and "Cookiewatch."

Hsu had previously worked at a stop-motion animation studio along with Justin Rasch, one of Blizzard's senior cinematic animators. Very few of their coworkers had any experience in the world of stop-motion animation, but they were fascinated by it. "Stop-motion is so cool," said character art director Arnold Tsang. "Any artist out there who doesn't do stop-motion is always amazed by stop-motion."

**LEFT** Justin Rasch poses a Reaper puppet used in the stop-motion animation "Trace & Bake."

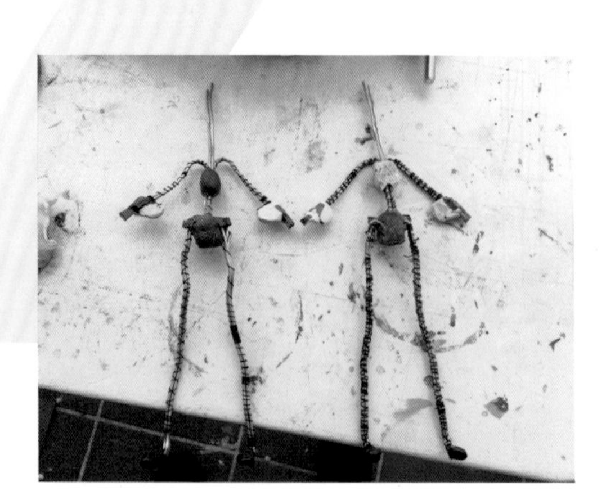

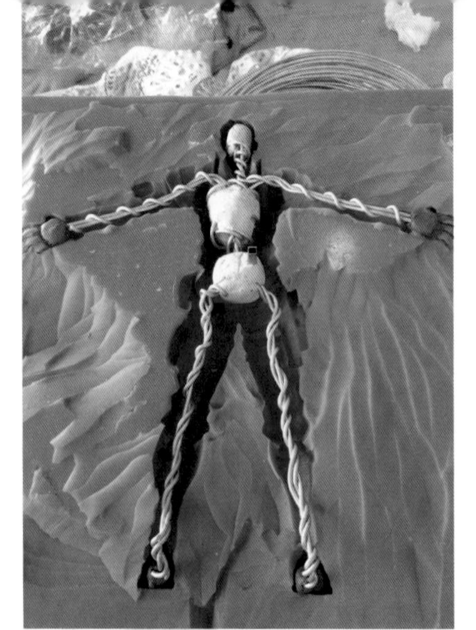

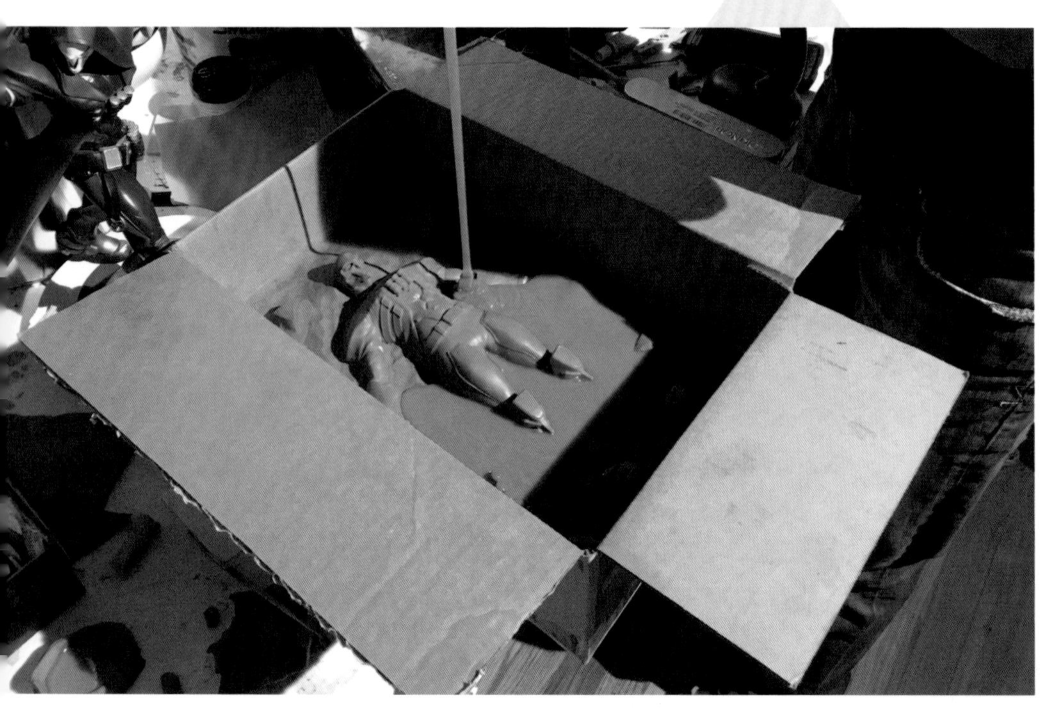

Many artists on campus shared Tsang's wonder with the medium and would approach Rasch with questions. "So ever since I joined Blizzard, people were like, 'There's a stop-motion guy here,'" said Rasch. "They kept asking me and being very curious, and then I was contacted by a few people saying I should teach a class."

During the course, Rasch couldn't help but make his own stop-motion project—a short featuring Soldier: 76 that showed a maquette of the character coming to life at night and trying to play *Overwatch* on a PC. "I thought, 'Wouldn't it be so funny if these maquettes came to life and played *Overwatch* at night? They had just given us the Soldier: 76 collectible figurine, and it wasn't far from being a puppet."

With some help from the sculpting team at Blizzard and his wife, Shel Wagner-Rasch, who builds stop-motion sets, Rasch made a secret film to show his class. "I didn't tell anyone about it," he said. "I just wanted to show the students at the end of the course and then share it with the other animators. Then people were like, 'You've got to show this to the rest of the team.' And they loved it."

From that moment on, there had to be an official Overwatch stop-motion animation short. It was just a matter of finding the right project.

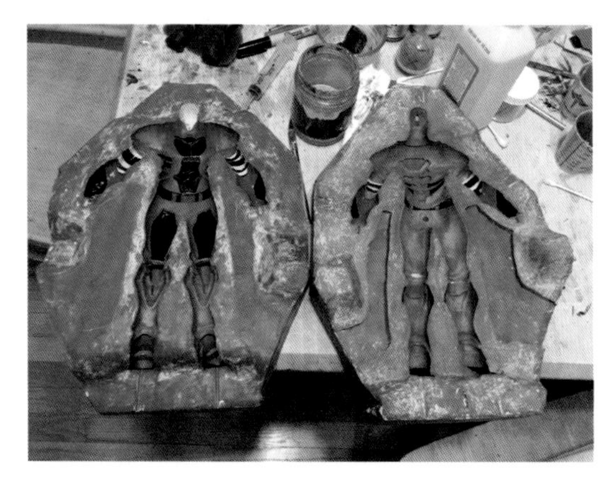

**THIS PAGE** Photographs of the process used to mold articulated silicone figures for stop-motion. Shel Wagner-Rasch pours the mold (top right).

**OPPOSITE** Work-in-progress Reaper (top left), Tracer (bottom left), and Doomfist (right) puppets.

## ONE SHOT AT A TIME

While shepherding the Overwatch characters through stop-motion production, Rasch was careful to honor the property and document everything he did, bringing the team into the process with regular reviews. "He did an awesome job translating this new format and making sure that we were true to the IP," said Hsu. "He did a whole bunch of tests that really impressed the team. Every time we would meet with them and show them the time lapses, they were just in awe because you could see how many times he changed outfits, which showed how many days had passed—just to get a tiny bit of footage."

Ultimately, the team was delighted to let Hsu and Rasch adapt their characters to the stop-motion medium. "At a certain point, there's a separation between the creator and the art, where it's like, 'This is bigger than any one of us,'" said Tsang. "It's not a sense of like, 'This is something I made, and somebody is changing it.' It's more like, 'Look at this crazy thing we made together, and look how it's affected people.'"

**ABOVE** The array of paints and paintbrushes Rasch and Wagner-Rasch used to finalize details for the character puppets.

**RIGHT** Still from the "Cookiewatch" stop-motion animation.

# TRACE & BAKE

"H-HELLO!
DO YOU KNOW WHAT TODAY IS?"

—TRACER

**"TRACE & BAKE"—RELEASED ON MAY 19, 2018—WAS A** special production meant to celebrate the second anniversary of *Overwatch*. Senior cinematic animator Justin Rasch pitched several ideas for the short, and the one that stuck was a story about Reaper and Tracer figurines coming to life to make a cake to commemorate the milestone.

"That was a pretty incredible moment," said *Overwatch*'s game director, Jeff Kaplan. "I remember just thinking to myself, 'Well, we need to figure out how we can get this made.' I've always felt like, in some ways, we're patrons of the arts. It's part of our responsibility, when we see something great and we see talented people like Justin, just to figure out how we can enable that."

Once Rasch got the concept approved, he started to develop his idea by photographing statues of Tracer and Reaper around his kitchen. These photographs served as reference and were eventually combined with storyboard images he drew to create a rough animatic. Rasch showed this to the team, got sign-off, and locked in his shot list.

Before any shots could be recorded, Rasch had to create models of the characters and build sets. For both tasks, he turned to his wife and fellow stop-motion practitioner, Shel Wagner-Rasch. The Blizzard sculpting team 3D printed models of Tracer and Reaper for them, which they used to cast silicone figures. Rasch and

**RIGHT** Still from the "Trace & Bake" stop-motion animation.

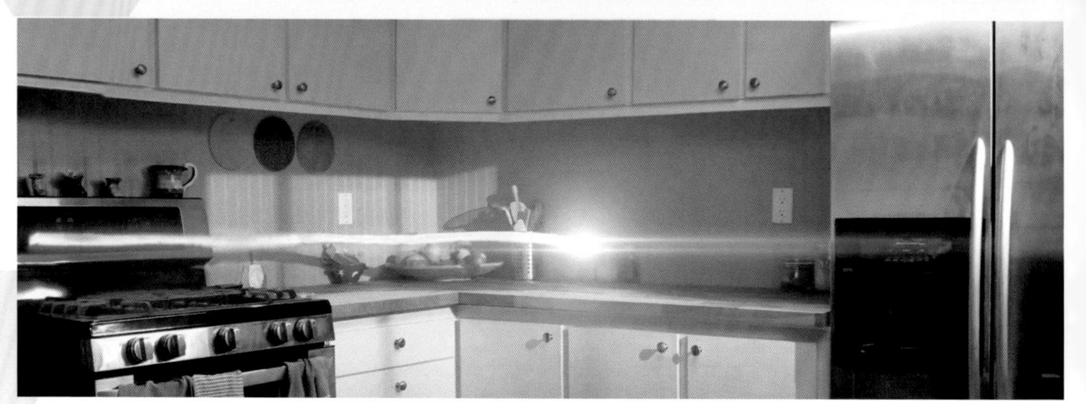

Wagner-Rasch then outfitted the maquettes with aluminum-wire rigging and attachments. Wagner-Rasch also built a kitchen set in their garage with removable surfaces and bolt holes throughout so that the figures could be anchored as they were repositioned between shots.

Working with physical characters and sets, stop-motion animation is a finite process that demands exacting attention for every shot. "In CG, you can block out your shot with just the poses that are the storytelling poses," said Rasch. "And then you can show the director and get feedback on that and then change it, and then slowly start to fill in the blanks with more information, refining the whole time. But with stop-motion, you get what you get at the end. That's part of the magic of it."

This became especially challenging when Rasch wanted to translate some of Overwatch CG animation's signature exaggeration to the intensely physical medium of stop-motion animation. "I can't do smears like we do in CG, like really getting a big blur," said Rasch. "But I was able to do some timing stuff that was a little more extreme than natural, realistic. When Reaper pulls out his guns, for example, we bent the nozzles of the weapons to make them seem a little bit looser and more flexible. To do that, I had about six different versions of the gun in various states of bending.

"And there are moments of hang time that are a little too long or moments of transition that are a little too fast. I kept some of that spacing and brought it directly over to my stop-motion timing. It's just one more element that makes it seem like Overwatch."

**TOP LEFT** *Overwatch* anniversary cake concept.

**TOP RIGHT** Reference photographs showing how Tracer's Blink ability was re-created using practical effects.

**OPPOSITE** Stills depicting the characters lighting the anniversary cake candles, which are actually LED lights with dimmer switches.

## DIFFERENT BUT THE SAME

Besides the cool factor, one of the things that made it easy for the team to enthusiastically endorse a stop-motion project was the way in which Hsu and Rasch positioned their depiction of the characters. "We're not saying that the characters in those pieces are the characters from the game or the storyline," said Hsu. "We're saying that they are statues that have come to life. They embody those characters but they exist outside of the game so we can play with them—like Reaper being a little bit more approachable."

"In a way, we were saying, 'These aren't your characters,'" said Rasch. "'They are like echoes that got stuck in some of the artistry that's come out of your world.' That gave me so much more leeway to have fun with them and slightly parody some of their personalities. I stayed true to them, but obviously, giving Reaper a sweet tooth is something that's off character, but it's fun, and it's still him. It's how far-reaching our universe can go—past the video game and out into the real world."

This license to play with the characters also extended to their physical representations, which sometimes had to be altered slightly to work with the medium. "The characters have to stay true to themselves, but we make little tweaks to adapt them to the stop-motion process," said Hsu. "For instance, hands and wrists are often the parts of puppets that need to be replaced quite often because of how small they are and how much action they need to do. We had to thicken up Tracer's wrists a bit because they were so delicate and would break too easily."

## *PRACTICAL EFFECTS*

▲ One of the biggest questions that arose during the production of "Trace & Bake" was how to pull off Tracer's Blink and Reaper's Wraith Form. Rasch wanted to do the effects practically, so he had to devise ways to translate the iconic CG visuals to reality.

"For Tracer's Blink, I used this blue medical tubing and put LED lights inside of it," said Rasch. "And then my wife made this sock that would go over it. And then I would frame-by-frame animate it, and we would cut off any of the wires supporting it and put a little flair on it in post.

"Reaper's Wraith Form is black witch's cotton. It's basically the stuff you make spider webs out of during Halloween, except it's black."

Arguably the most impressive effect in the short are the candles on the cake. "My wife made these fake candles and we put little LED lights in them with dimmers so I could adjust them frame by frame and make them appear to flicker," said Rasch. ▼

# COOKIEWATCH

"SANTA NEVER CAME TO MY HOUSE."

—REAPER

**LIKE "TRACE & BAKE," "COOKIEWATCH"—RELEASED ON** December 18, 2018—centered around sweet baked goods and was tied to a celebration. This set a precedent of sorts—that for Overwatch, stop-motion was going to be linked to joyful events, a take counter to the more foreboding subject matter usually explored in the medium. "Typically, I would say that stop-motion has really dark themes," said producer Emily Hsu. "Which the Overwatch stop-motion cinematics don't have at all. They are fun and playful. So they're maybe countering traditional stop-motion themes and motifs, in a way."

A lot of that has to do with senior cinematic animator Justin Rasch's positive personality and his love of holidays, particularly Christmas. "I wanted to do Christmas so bad," said Rasch. "I actually had 'Cookiewatch' boarded before I did 'Trace & Bake.'"

Rasch had been working independently on the project, shooting time-lapse reference, before it was green-lighted. Once it became official, he was able to spend twelve solid weeks on the project. "I got to have Christmas for three months before Christmas!" he said.

One of the main goals of "Cookiewatch" was to introduce another character into the stop-motion mix: Doomfist. As with Tracer and Reaper before, Rasch wanted to make sure to feature one of Doomfist's signature special abilities using practical effects. "Anytime we bring a new character into one of these shorts, we try to solve their special abilities practically," said Rasch. "So for

**RIGHT** The final shot in "Cookiewatch" where the characters examine their presents from Santa.

Fr: Santa

Doomfist, we did his Meteor Strike. In the game, it's a big tube that comes down, and then it gets a little larger, and then he smashes it. For the practical effect, we got a bunch of lighting paper, which we made into a blue tube, and we put the reticle on there to get the shape on the ground when we shined a light through."

Because Rasch had already delivered big on "Trace & Bake," the Overwatch team committed additional talent to help with "Cookiewatch," particularly for effects and lighting. A prime example is the way the glass of milk ripples when Doomfist smashes down. "With the support of the Blizzard Cinematics FX and Lighting teams, we really upped the bar in terms of quality and quantity of effects and lighting, which you can see when you compare 'Cookiewatch' with 'Trace & Bake,'" said Hsu.

Effects also helped when there were little slips in continuity. "You're not shooting in sequential order," said Hsu. "You're shooting in whatever order makes sense for the production based on practical sets and puppet builds. So even tracking things like a cookie, there are things that get missed. Reshooting anything in stop-motion is incredibly time-consuming and laborious so we can sometimes make the call to fix or hide things in postproduction."

With the broader team effort on "Cookiewatch," Overwatch solidified a commitment to stop-motion animation as a medium in its storytelling mix. "At this point, Overwatch is the only franchise at Blizzard that has made the foray into stop-motion," said Hsu.

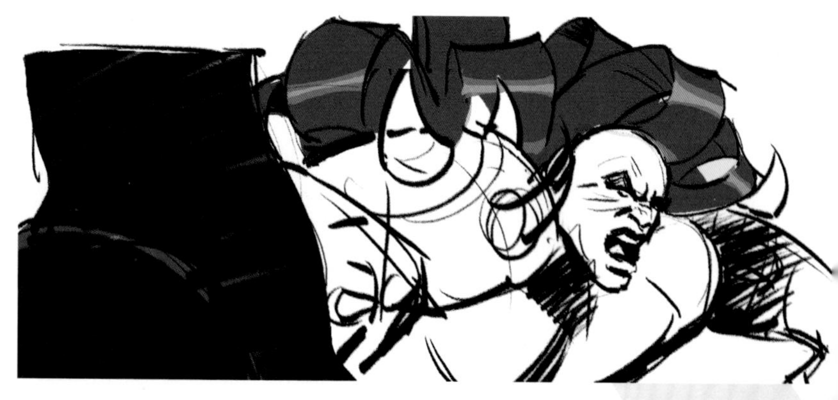

**THESE PAGES** Storyboards created to visualize the setting and action.

### STICKER MOUTHS

▲ Animating mouths to make it look like characters are speaking is particularly tricky in stop-motion animation. For Reaper, with his full-face mask, this wasn't really an issue, but Doomfist and Tracer were another matter. Rather than doing full animation with replacement faces, Rasch opted for a relatively low-impact technique, sticker mouths.

"You work out your facial stuff before you go to the set," said Rasch. "Because we were just doing sticker mouths, I would take the audio file, and I would do the images, changing the mouth shapes. Basically, I had a list and it said, 'On frame 16, it has to be an M-shaped mouth; for 18, it has to be an O-shaped mouth.'"

"The mouths don't animate like they would in a 3D cinematic, but the medium lends itself to a certain level of imperfection," said Hsu. "That's also part of what makes it really lovely and relatable." ▼

A-07
LOREM REST
Boulangerie
La Boulangerie
La Boulangerie

# CONCLUSION

SIX

**AFTER “REUNION,” THE TEAM BEGAN WORKING ON A CINEMATIC TO ANNOUNCE *OVERWATCH 2* CALLED “ZERO HOUR,” WHICH WAS RELEASED ON NOVEMBER 1, 2019,** at BlizzCon. The filmmakers knew that expectations would be high. They not only had to convey all the promise of *Overwatch 2,* which would include new character designs, plots, and locations, but also resolve the defining narrative arc of the prerendered cinematics they had produced to date.

“We tried to tie up as many loose ends as we could from the previous shorts,” said director Ben Dai. “We knew Mei was on her way to find Winston, Tracer answers the call right away, and Reinhart and Brigitte as well. In ‘Dragons,’ we hinted that Genji was a strong possibility. And McCree set things in motion for Echo.”

Mercy was the only character in "Zero Hour" who didn’t have an animated short, but fans had seen her reaction to the recall and her own reawakening to heroism in the “Valkyrie” short story.

LEFT Final render of Winston facing off against the giant mech in “Zero Hour.”

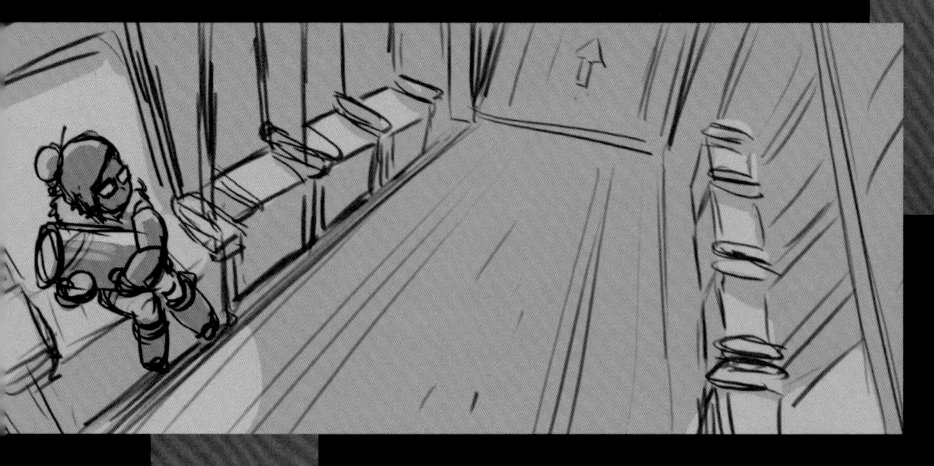

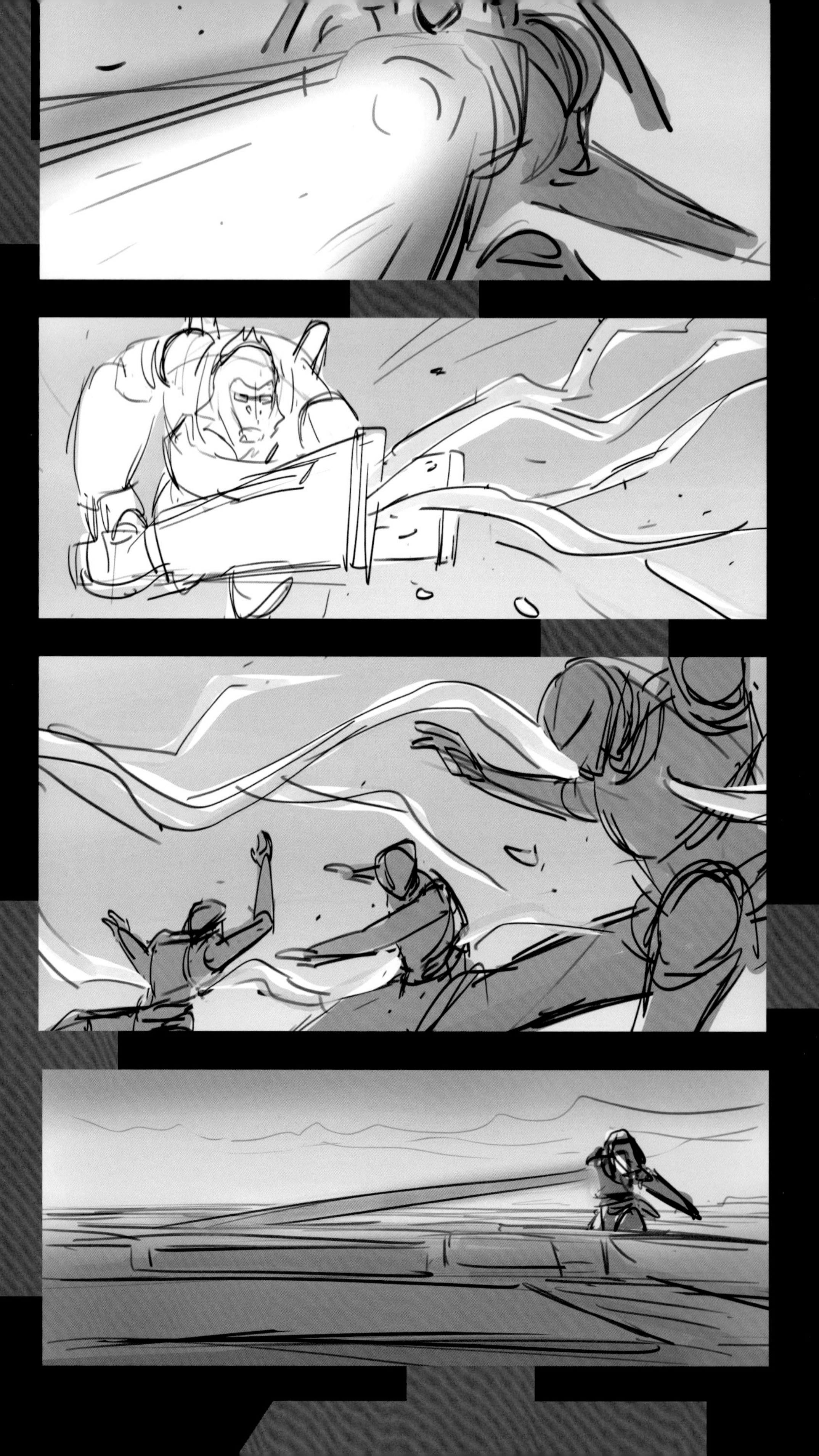

Besides showing how the heroes answered Winston's call, "Zero Hour" also had to tee up the new story the team planned to tell in *Overwatch 2*. "It's the handoff back to the game," said senior producer Kevin VanderJagt. "Up until this point, Overwatch existed as a transmedia experience. It was comic books. It was our Overwatch shorts. You had to go out and find the story. *Overwatch 2* is taking that mantle back and will now be the main narrative driver for the Overwatch world. 'Zero Hour' handed that baton back to the game. The story is now the game story; it's no longer this meta story that we've been telling."

With so much riding on "Zero Hour," the team wanted to set the bar higher, hinting at the level of attention, craft, and quality that would be inherent to everything—cinematics, comics, games, other media—released under the banner of *Overwatch 2*. "It had to feel like the culmination of everything we had done as a studio, from the effects to character looks, shading, lighting—all plussed to a new level," said Anthony Eftekhari, the cinematic's

**THESE PAGES** Storyboards depicting key moments in the animated short.

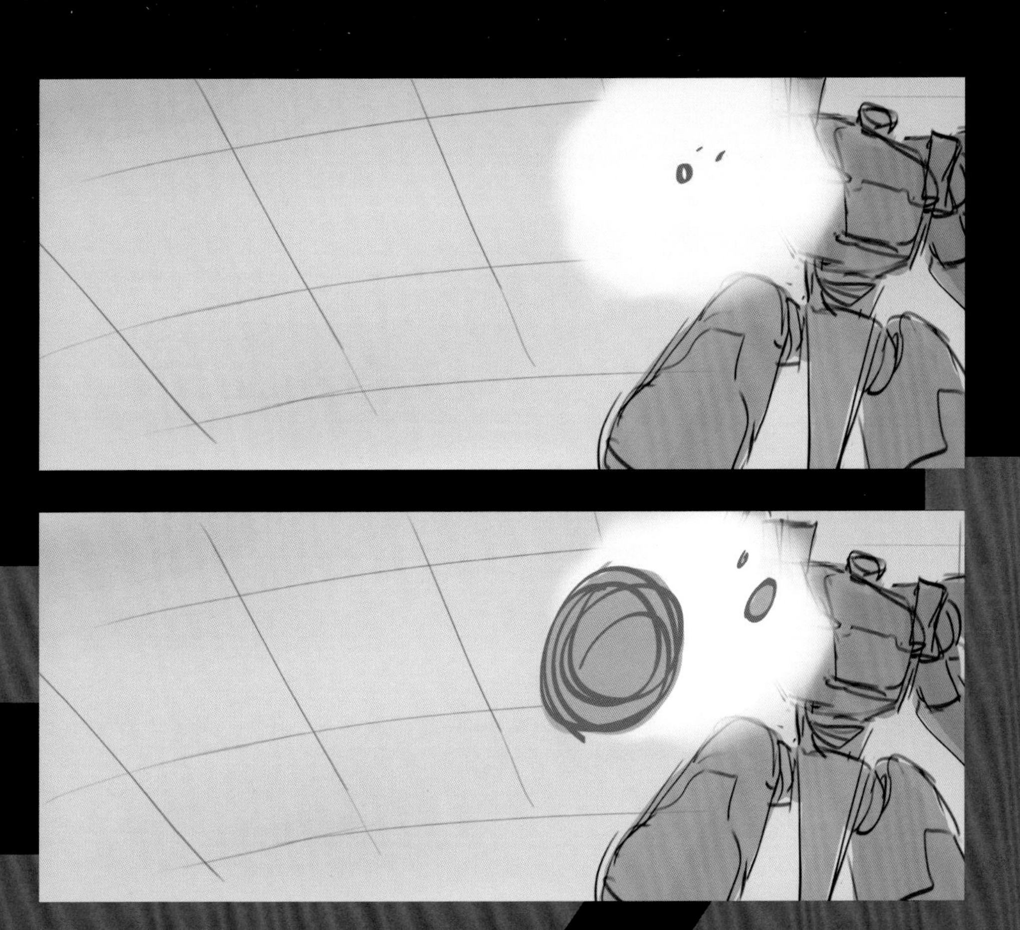

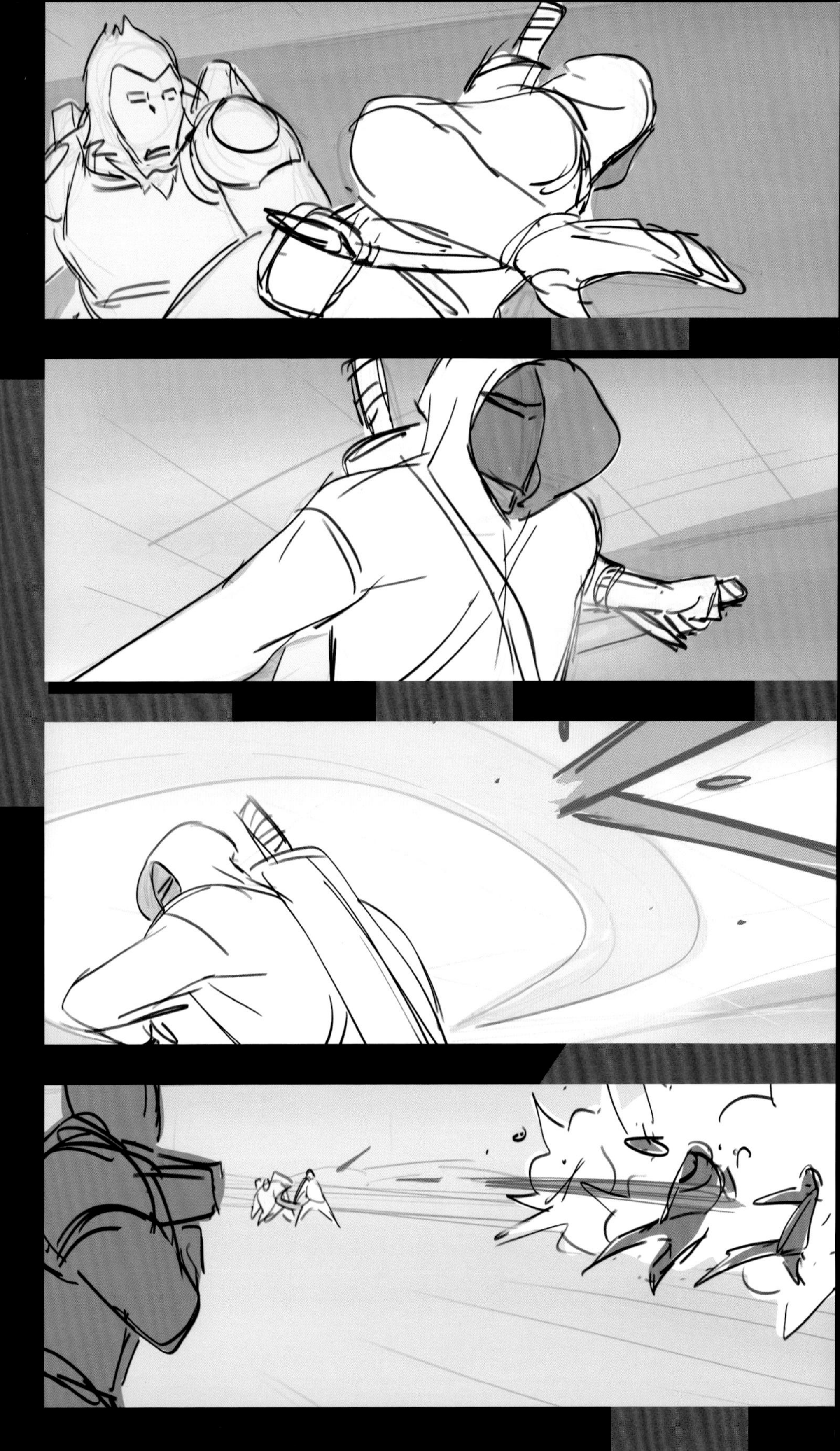

art director. "So we wanted the sets to be more elaborate. The destruction in Paris had to feel grittier, a little bit bigger. And there were higher-fidelity characters who all got new outfits with better shading and texturing and more intricate details. It had to feel new; it had to feel 2.0."

Both a fitting finale and an ambitious new beginning, "Zero Hour" would hint at the scope of the cinematic storytelling planned for *Overwatch 2*. While the game would become the main storytelling vehicle with the second release, that didn't mean the animated shorts, 2.5D motion stories, stop-motion animation, and other formats would be forgotten.

Quite the contrary: the diverse visual storytelling vehicles the Overwatch team had developed over the years would continue to be just as important and would be used to embellish and explore the world outside the game. And with what was coming next, the filmmakers were determined to continue pushing Overwatch cinematics to new heights of artistic and technical quality.

With *Overwatch 2*, Overwatch was about to get a whole lot bigger, and so were the cinematic stories the team was planning to tell . . .

**OPPOSITE** Concept of the giant mech.

**THIS PAGE** Storyboards of Genji's arrival.

**FOLLOWING PAGES** Final render of the last shot in the film.

08

WRITTEN BY JAKE GERLI
LEAD EDITOR MATT BURNS
ART DIRECTION BETSY PETERSCHMIDT
LORE CONSULTATION MADI BUCKINGHAM, SEAN COPELAND, JUSTIN PARKER, ANNE STICKNEY
PRODUCTION CHLOE FRABONI, BRIANNE MESSINA, DEREK ROSENBERG, DAVID SEEHOLZER, ANNA WAN
DIRECTOR, CONSUMER PRODUCTS BYRON PARNELL

THIS PAGE Final illustration from the Wrecking Ball origin story.

PAGE 1 Illustration of the Deadlock Gang from the Ashe origin story.

PAGES 2–3 Render of D.Va.

PAGE 4 Color key of the train wreck in the "Reunion" animated short.

PAGES 6–7 Render of Reinhardt.

SPECIAL THANKS
TED BOONTHANAKIT, ROBERT BROOKS, JEFF CHAMBERLAIN, STEVEN CHEN, MICHAEL CHU, SHIMON COHEN, BEN DAI, MIO DEL ROSARIO, ANTHONY EFTEKHARI, HUNTER GRANT, DOUG GREGORY, JASON HILL, EMILY HSU, JIM JIANG, JERAMIAH JOHNSON, JEFF KAPLAN, MIKE KOIZUMI, GEORGE KRSTIC, YUI KURITA, TIM LOUGHRAN, NESSKAIN, RACHEL RICHMOND, ANDREW ROBINSON, DION ROGERS, ARNOLD TSANG, KEVIN VANDERJAGT, MATHIAS VERHASSELT



Published by Titan Books, London, in 2021.

Published by arrangement with Blizzard Entertainment, Inc., Irvine, California.



**TITAN** BOOKS
A division of Titan Publishing Group Ltd
144 Southwark Street. London SE1 0UP
www.titanbooks.com
Find us on Facebook: www.facebook.com/titanbooks
Follow us on Twitter: @TitanBooks

A CIP catalogue record for this title is available from the British Library.

ISBN: 9781789097504

Printed in China

BOOK DESIGN BY **CAMERON + COMPANY**
PUBLISHER CHRIS GRUENER
CREATIVE DIRECTOR IAIN R. MORRIS
DESIGNER ROB DOLGAARD

9 8 7 6 5 4 3 2 1

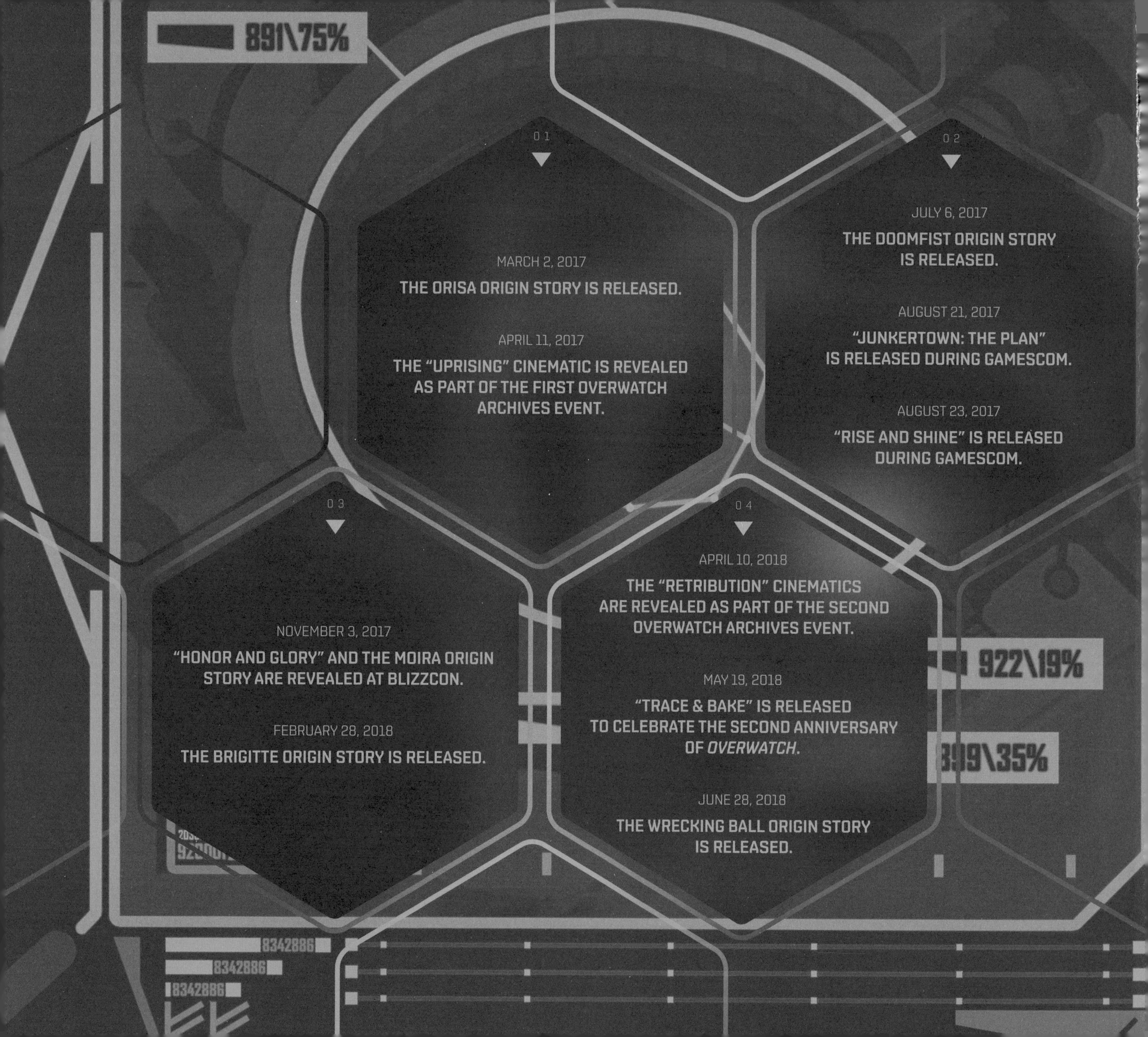
891\75%
01
MARCH 2, 2017
THE ORISA ORIGIN STORY IS RELEASED.
APRIL 11, 2017
THE "UPRISING" CINEMATIC IS REVEALED AS PART OF THE FIRST OVERWATCH ARCHIVES EVENT.
02
JULY 6, 2017
THE DOOMFIST ORIGIN STORY IS RELEASED.
AUGUST 21, 2017
"JUNKERTOWN: THE PLAN" IS RELEASED DURING GAMESCOM.
AUGUST 23, 2017
"RISE AND SHINE" IS RELEASED DURING GAMESCOM.
03
NOVEMBER 3, 2017
"HONOR AND GLORY" AND THE MOIRA ORIGIN STORY ARE REVEALED AT BLIZZCON.
FEBRUARY 28, 2018
THE BRIGITTE ORIGIN STORY IS RELEASED.
04
APRIL 10, 2018
THE "RETRIBUTION" CINEMATICS ARE REVEALED AS PART OF THE SECOND OVERWATCH ARCHIVES EVENT.
MAY 19, 2018
"TRACE & BAKE" IS RELEASED TO CELEBRATE THE SECOND ANNIVERSARY OF *OVERWATCH*.
JUNE 28, 2018
THE WRECKING BALL ORIGIN STORY IS RELEASED.
922\19%
899\35%
8342886
8342886
8342886